YOUR WORLD IMPACT

AS A FINANCIAL ADVISOR

....

IMPACT YOUR WORLD

Rebuild Your Financial Practice and
Protect Your Clients from Themselves

....

TYSON JON RAY

YOUR WORLD IMPACT

Copyright © 2012 by
Children's World Impact Foundation
(Children's World Impact, Inc.)

Because of the dynamic nature of the Internet, any Web addresses or links contained in this book may have changed since publication and may no longer be valid.

DISCLOSURE: With the exception of my family and authority references, names have been changed to protect the privacy of my clients. Identifying details of any interactions with clients or actual events involving clients have been altered to protect their privacy. They still convey true lessons learned from those interactions or events. In no way should any advice given or action recommended in this book be construed to guarantee any specific outcome, income, or result.

Editing and Production Assistance by Elizabeth H. Cottrell of RiverwoodWriter.com

Photography by Ryan Bensheimer of Idealimpressions.com

Graphic Design by Julie Nor of FlairStudio.net

Coaching by Sheri Burnham of LidLifterInc.com

Printed in the United States of America

www.yourworldimpact.com

DEDICATION:

Aside from my faith and my wife Jenny, there are three
individuals who have impacted me the most in my life
and my role as a financial advisor.
I don't know where they stop and I start.

Nick Murray
Bob Dunwoody
Duncan MacPherson

Thank you.

PRAISE FOR *YOUR WORLD IMPACT*:

"*Your World Impact* has a deep and powerful message: know yourself, know your role and know your client. It manages to touch upon these issues deeply and with genuine integrity. The world needs a new type of financial advisor, and this book challenges the reader to truly live up to the noble calling of this profession. I highly recommend it!"

– Tim Ursiny, Ph.D., CBC, RCC
CEO of Advantage Coaching
www.advantagecoaching.com

"This is an excellent quick read for financial advisors interested in navigating themselves and their practices in a successful direction. The book articulates key practice management concepts in a heartwarming personal way."

– Gene Diederich
CEO Moneta Group
www.monetagroup.com

"This is a must-read for the financial advisor or any person who would like to learn how to play rather than work. Come see how a book can put you on the path towards yourself. Not the person you were, not the person you are, but the person you were meant to be."

– Bob Dunwoody
Speaker, author & founder of Productivity, Inc.
www.bobdunwoody.com

"This is one of the great success stories in the profession of financial advice. This book is simple, human and above all personal. It is testimony to the profound truth that advisors can only do well by doing good."

– Nick Murray,
Speaker, author and founder The Nick Murray Company, Inc.
www.nickmurray.com

"Many books have been written on the topic of advisor productivity. *Your World Impact* stands out because it not only helps you aspire to new levels of achievement, but it also provides you with an actionable approach to balanced success at home and in business. This proven process and these time-tested principles will help you get to that next level and keep you focused on what really matters in life."

– Duncan MacPherson
Co-Founder of Pareto Systems
www.paretosystems.com

TABLE OF CONTENTS

PREFACE:
You Value Them

Why You Need to Read this Book

Ready, fire, aim…

Funny how often in life we run off taking action before we really know where we are going or how best to get there.

I decided to write this book because I want to help people—that includes both you and your clients—do what I believe they cannot do by themselves. The purpose of this book is to help you (the financial advisor) be your best self, create more value (through your financial practice) to help them (your clients) achieve their dreams and goals. When you improve the quality of life for yourself and your clients, you impact the world.

If you value them, they will value you.

I'm not preaching any type of get rich quick scheme for either you or your clients. I'm talking about a way of behaving and a way of doing business that is people- and value-centric. I have seen these principles produce dramatic results for my own practice and that of others. By implementing them, I believe you can:

- Turn lukewarm clients into devoted followers and even raging fans.
- Turn a high stress financial practice into one that is both meaningful and manageable.
- Turn your advice to clients into win-win propositions without sacrificing your integrity or your income and without compromising their financial well-being.
- Stop being a salesperson and start being a trusted advisor.
- Stop stressing out about finding the next best investment.
- Find comfort in knowing you've done your best for your clients and that you're not chasing yesterday's returns.
- Free up more time for your personal dreams and goals while adding more value to helping your clients achieve theirs.
- Take the emphasis off making more money and put it on goal attainment.

Life in "The Dash"

Early in my career, I had an interesting day. It was a day in which I attended both a baptism and a funeral. The baby was my newest client. After his birth and receiving a Social Security number, a college savings plan was started for that child. I was invited to the church to attend the baptism and celebrate the newness of life and the commitment of that life to the Lord. Seeing how the family celebrated brought a wonderful perspective of the purity of how we enter this world and what life is all about.

Ironically, I walked out of that church, across Main Street, and into another church to attend a client's funeral. There I watched a family mourn and remember a life that had been lived. As I sat on a pew during the service reading the dates of this person's life, 1921-2002, I realized something.

My life, my clients' lives, and the life of each person I impact can be summed up in that dash—the dash between birth and death. Your whole life is lived between two sets of numbers.

My life started in 1975 and will end in 20??. In fact, everyone who is old enough to be in this business is going to die in 20??. So, there is one known number and one unknown number, and then your life in between.

The reality of "the dash" became very clear to me that day. Despite the fact that those two dates, birth and death, are specific dates in time, we don't have a lot of control over those actual numbers. What we do with our lives, however—the dash in between those two numbers—is something we can focus on. That is something we can influence.

That realization defined for me what my job is really all about. My job is to enhance the dash in my clients' lives as much as possible. My passion is to help people do more, to reach their greatest potential and in doing so, to maximize their impact on this world. What I discovered later is that when I do this to the best of my ability, I enhance the dash in my own life as well.

This book is a continuation of my effort to impact this world by helping you, my fellow professionals, to impact the lives of people who trust you with their entire life savings. I want to see us do it right. I see many advisors, though, who are screwing it up. They're doing more damage to their clients than anything else, and I think I have figured out how to fix that.

The Urgent versus the Important

I believe that deep down, financial advisors are hard-wired to do what's right by their clients. The problem is, the belief system we have been taught often works against the clients' long-term interests. I want financial advisors to start learning and teaching the right things—many of which they innately know—and debunk some of the many wrong teachings that exist in the financial world. I believe a person's lived life is more important than money. The things money can't buy—love, integrity, time, experience, family, and peace of mind—are the things that we are seeking in life.

This book is to help the advisor in you realize your job is not to make people money but to help your clients use their money to make more of a life.

It may sound simple, but most advisors focus solely on the money in accounts, the markets and economic events, rather than on the life of the client. Too often, they let the "urgent crowd out the important." This book is designed to help you realize that the "urgent" issues we too often focus on have too much to do with things we can neither control nor change. The urgent issues often go from topic to topic, creating a social drug to heighten your fears and justify going against both history and facts. We have got to stop focusing on the urgent and start focusing on what's important.

The problem with society is that as a collective, the things we believe and do around the topic of money lead to a "herd" mentality. In the herd, individuals feel they must do what everyone else is doing without considering the consequences of that choice and whether that choice is in alignment with what they want to accomplish in life. Herd mentality is dangerous. As a young financial advisor, I started out with the herd mentality and quickly discovered that it was the quickest way to financial ruin, not success. Everyone is usually wrong at the same time everyone else is wrong. This makes being wrong feel so right, and makes being right so hard because everyone else is wrong.

The Tragedy of Herd Mentality

I saw first-hand the devastating damage the Herd has on our advice and our clients' decisions. One poignant example is Mary Jane. Mary Jane came to me in 2000. She had worked 40 years as a clerk at JC Penney and finally decided to retire. She squirreled away $122,000 in a 401K. This $122,000 was all the money she and Dick had besides their Social Security checks. Due to a union classification, Mary Jane wasn't eligible for a pension. Despite saving for 40 years, the dollars had not grown because no one told her she was investing in a money market all the years she had it. When she realized this, Mary Jane was determined to start growing her money. "Everyone is making money on their savings besides me," she exclaimed, "I want to own technology investments; that's where the money is." Indeed at that time, tech stocks were performing well, and I researched her options. At the time, CNBC and the financial media seemed to believe 100% growth stocks, specifically technology, was the only place to be. The media created the phrase the "New Economy," and they implied this was the only way to invest in the future. So, I invested her savings in the growth strategy she wanted. It felt good. Mary Jane was happy and so was I. Everyone got what they wanted. Besides, I assumed that if I didn't do what she wanted, I would lose the sale. She might go to the advisor next door, and he would sell her what she thought she wanted. I figured I might as well get paid and provide the service rather than lose the sale by talking her into something else. I know now, however, that the few hundred dollars I made were not worth the long-term life-changing damage that unfolded.

Within a year, the entire picture had changed. First, the tech bubble burst with a two year market decline, and Mary Jane lost fully half of everything she saved over 40 years. Then, Dick got sick and prescriptions were expensive. Their Social Security checks, which they were counting on to cover their living expenses, were not enough. Over the next two years, they spent their savings down to nothing. Then, Dick died. Mary Jane was a widow on a single Social Security check with medical bills to pay. I was haunted knowing she would live in this state for the rest of her life.

Poverty stinks. Our advice to our clients can help them avoid it or take them directly to it. I believe that with the advice in this book, you can significantly increase the odds that you'll not only help them avoid it, but help enhance the quality of their lives significantly. This is not pie-in-the-sky, feel-good advice. It is based on numbers and my own hard-fought experience and that of others.

Mary Jane and Dick's story is sad. The real tragedy is that it happens all the time. It happens when people make choices because it "feels good" at the time. I made a promise to myself in 2002 that I would not allow myself to make an investment for a client simply because it "feels good" or because it is what everyone thinks is the "right choice" or because the client wants me to do it. I will recommend what I believe to be best for the client every time, even if it is not what they want, and even if it means less money for me. If you think this sounds like professional suicide, let me tell you why I feel so strongly about this, because I learned it the hard way:

I know it is better to forego a commission or fee generated for the wrong reason than to bear the guilt and shame of having allowed someone to follow a path straight to their own destruction.

Wants versus Needs and Knowing Yourself

Here is a fact: People end up being pretty poor clients if they run out of money—literally and figuratively!

I am writing this book to keep you from making mistakes and to teach you how to find a more valuable alternative than giving people only what they want. It is giving them what they need. I hope to convince you that more often than not, being a financial advisor is about helping people do what they may not want to do and help them from doing what it is they think they want to do. To accomplish this, you must first really understand yourself and your values to have the internal fortitude and foundation for this critical work.

The Choice: Debt or Legacy?

Every person, without exception, is going to either outlive their money—e.g., run out, ending up like Mary Jane in my example above—or their money will outlive them, thus leaving a legacy. After learning how it feels to have a client run out of money because of bad decisions which could have been avoided, I am now on a mission to do all I can to help make sure that we, as professionals in the financial services industry, do not let that happen again.

Please do not misread my message here. I am not saying it's wrong to invest in the markets or that Mary Jane should not have put her retirement into a long-term, asset-allocated, diversified and rebalanced portfolio. In my opinion, that is exactly what she should have done, because if she had, she would still have it or at least some of it. Rather, what I am saying is that I should not have allowed the CNBC, Mad Money, hot ideas that come from the herd running wild to affect my judgment, my practice or my integrity. We can't allow these short-term distractions to affect our long-term value and our clients' lives.

INTRODUCTION:
The End

....

How do you want to be remembered? What do you want people to say about you at your funeral?

Between today and that day, you can choose to live in a way that affects how your life is viewed in the end. Who you are and what you do creates the narrative for your life and will inform what is said about you at your funeral. I am not trying to be morbid, but I want you to remember this guiding principle:

Start with the End in Mind

When you embark upon a journey, if you first know where you want to go, the best path will become clear. I want you to become a person who values yourself, values your clients, and values the process required to keep adding value. We will build a business model around that process and help you share it with others.

I believe this book will help you stand out from the crowd. You'll learn to differentiate yourself from the herd of financial advisors offering the better investment strategy, the better portfolio, the better idea, and the better trade. Instead you'll seek to be a person whose clients will come to your funeral and speak highly of you, because you've made a difference in their lives. In order to do this you must have integrity. Integrity generates energy. Integrity only comes when you know who you are, a topic we'll explore in the "Part You" section of this book. You must add value to the process. You must find people who want the value you add. You cannot be everything to everybody, so stop right now and get your bearings. You're about to discover a different map—a map that will guide you on your path to security and peace of mind.

We'll start with the ancient wisdom of Socrates, "Know Thyself." In order to understand "You," we are going to explore who you really are, what you believe, how to give of yourself, and how people want to connect with you.

Investing is No Place for Emotion

Investors are emotional creatures, not often logical. Their emotion leads them to exit the market after losing money and enter the market after they see it appreciate. It is amazing that they understand buying summer clothes in winter and winter clothes in the summer because they are half off, but many don't understand it is counterintuitive to buy low and sell high within their investment portfolio. Rather than buy low and sell high, most clients buy high, hoping it goes higher and sell low in fear it will go lower. That is like selling their swimsuit in a blizzard and using the money to buy a winter jacket when its price is high because of demand, then selling the winter jacket six months later in the middle of a heat wave when the demand is very low.

It may sound silly, but silly becomes serious when advisors do not counsel against making emotion-driven decisions. And serious becomes dangerous when the broker encourages emotional decisions to drive sales and generate compensation for himself. The unfortunate consequence may be a large and painful loss to the client.

Desired Result: Life Improvement

In my opinion, the current industry sales model is broken, and the average investor needs a different kind of advisor. Too many stockbrokers are salesmen trying to hide behind the title of financial advisor. Far too often, a broker peddles financial products and information about these products for compensation without any real vested interest in how the product fits, benefits or works for the client long term. If it doesn't work out and the client loses, the broker is still likely to get paid.

I don't want to be a broker. I don't want you to be a broker. I want us all to be trusted advisors for our clients' life savings. In this book, I am going to help you do this by exploring how to help clients the way they need to be helped. My goal is to teach you how to help make your clients better off than when you found them.

The bottom line is that sometimes our role as financial advisors is to help clients behave differently. We must hold their hand through the ups and downs of the market so they don't miss out on the potential returns nor sell and lock in permanent losses at the wrong times. This book is to help you realize one of the best hand-holding tools available is a plan: a document or record which reflects what the client's long-term stated goals and objectives are, and what they are not. The best way to add value is to have a plan in place and execute that plan over the course of their lifetime, helping to ensure that the long-term desires of the client prevail when the same clients' emotions dictate short-term decisions that are not conducive to achieving the long-term goals.

So what are you bringing to the table to add value to your clients? What is your "value add?"

Without clarifying the value we add, too many in our industry have been selling yesterday's winning lotto numbers for a fee. In doing so, we encourage clients to use past performance to make future decisions without having any idea what the money is for. In my opinion, this strategy cannot be executed with integrity. Integrity calls for you to really understand what your client's money is needed or wanted for. Your greatest "value add" is to help them understand what their money is for and then put a plan in place to help achieve their lifetime goals. Sticking to a well-designed plan is something we can control.

If your "value add" is to make your clients feel good about their emotional decisions, it may result in long-term regret. Most clients need an advisor who understands behavior management, not just money management. Clients should pay us to develop a plan, monitor a plan, and help them stick to a plan, rather than focusing strictly on the investments of a plan or paying us to just appease them into potentially making a long-term mistake.

We need to understand some practical truths:

- We've got to shift away from a sole focus on investment-based returns and market performance and help clients achieve financial goals. That's really what is important to them anyway.
- We must realize we are not in the money-making business; we are in the life improvement business.

It starts with asking and continuing to ask yourself and your clients this question: "What is the money for?"

Once you choose the path of integrity and value, disciplined business processes are required. Therefore, this book provides practical ideas on how to structure your business, service your clients, and while we are at it, help you get new ones who value and appreciate your approach to their needs.

History Lessons on Investing in Optimism

Before I go any further, I want to frame the reality of our past. The facts show clearly that optimism is the truest realism. In other words, we have been misled and ill-advised when we let fear and nervousness from short-term events or headlines rob us of the potential for long-term gain.

No one taught me this more than my oldest client Chris who died at age 98.

Chris was born in 1907, at a time when more than half of all US workers engaged in food production, half of all homes had no plumbing, and barely a third of the population had a high school diploma. There were almost no cars or radios, and the average life expectancy at birth was only 47.

Twenty years later, when Chris's son, Nelson, was born in 1927, the US was in the throes of industrialization, and with it, traditional farm life was on the decline. Cars and machinery replaced horse power, almost everyone had a radio, and Edison's genius was recognized with his inventions of the phonograph and light bulb. World War I was over, and with the country's improved health standards, life expectancy had increased to over 60 years of age.

Ironically, despite the many innovations during Chris's early life that saved time and money, and the fact that Americans were increasingly able to afford them, few people wanted to invest in America or the American economy. The wringer washing machine, electric lights, electric streetcars and vacuum cleaners were all greeted with fascination and excitement. But skepticism was still strong, and the risks of investing were considered too great.

In the 1920's, advances through human ingenuity brought production and prosperity to both American agriculture and industry. Even though human ingenuity gave birth to greater productivity, there remained a hesitancy to invest in the American economy during Nelson's youth as well. Before Nelson was out of knee pants, the equity market had declined 89%. For the first fifteen years of years of his life, America faced a prolonged depression, and a second World War. Many people were caught up in all of the negatives society was enduring. People still failed to invest appropriately.

The very real pain and distress of the Great Depression became embedded in the psyche of the survivors of that era. Depression stories and myths were passed from one generation to another. The result was that many investment decisions were based on these enduring myths. Today, retirement-age adults continue to make investment decisions based on conditions that occurred between seven and eight decades ago and may no longer be relevant.

The Great Depression hurt those who sold their investments based on fear, emotion or necessity. The few investors who were patient, however— and who kept their assets allocated among different asset classes, remained diversified inside those asset classes, and reinvested their dividends—made their investment loss back within a decade or shortly thereafter. In time, these savvy and steadfast investors actually went back to being permanently ahead.

The progress and growth that occurred after World War II should have created an ideal time to invest, but the lingering uncertainties from the 1930s still prevailed. If someone had invested $1,000 in the Standard & Poor's Index on January 2, 1945 when the modern stock market began, that investment would be worth over a million dollars today. I wonder how many soldiers returning from WWII would be leaving rich legacies today if they had just taken that plunge.

My client Chris was born during the horse and buggy days, but her grandson Austin was born in 1957, the same year that Voyager and Sputnik were launched. Most homes had indoor plumbing, and polio vaccine and penicillin rid the world of many scourges. The Cold War was in full swing, but the economy stalled in mid-1957, and few wanted to invest then. What if they had invested in 1957?

When Austin was born, the S&P 500 was right at 47, and the nation's GDP was over 465 billion. In less than 20 years, when Austin graduated from high school in 1975, both had nearly doubled. Still, any potential enthusiasm for investing was dampened by a recent recession, an oil embargo, and the disastrous consequences of double-digit inflation. Even with the virtually unknown innovation of the microprocessor in the early 1970s, few had an appetite for investing.

Austin's son, Carson, Chris's great grandchild, was born on December 17, 1979. On that day, the S&P closed at 107, and the nation's GDP was about 2.6 trillion. In spite of capitalism's steady growth, media headlines were discouraging, and people remained extremely conservative. Only those who ignored that negative drumbeat and invested anyway would have enjoyed the incredible leap forward that occurred in the stock market. With the development of microchip technology, and the destruction of the Berlin Wall in 1989, the S&P reached 1257 in 2008, and the GDP grew to more than 14.2 trillion. With the crumbling of Communism, new free markets emerged and grew. And America was at the forefront of all these changes.

The lesson here is so much more than just a finger wag at those afraid to take risks. History has clearly shown that optimism—even in the face of negative events and circumstances—has prevailed time and time again, as men and women choose their own destinies with creativity, grit and determination, just as our founding fathers did. Even though past performance cannot predict future results, it doesn't pay to bet against history.

Getting to know Chris taught me a lot about the power of optimism. Let's recap:

- 1957 – S&P was at 47 – US GDP $466 Billion
- 1975 – S&P was at 95 – US GDP $1.6 Trillion
- 2008 – S&P was at 1257 – US GDP $14.2 Trillion

Now here is what's amazing: There are over 70 million baby boomers who were born between 1946 and 1964, and many of these "boomers" still have an opinion that you cannot make money investing the in the markets. The media has repeatedly referred to the years between 2000 and 2010 as the lost decade, insinuating that investing doesn't work anymore. Much worse, there are advisors today who have the opinion that you can't make money investing in the markets over the long term. There is a stinking thinking going on that long-term investing should be replaced with short-term market timing. I believe the facts remain clear, however, that the most valuable investment, providing the greatest potential for increase in one's lifetime, with the least dilution to purchasing power and the lowest risk of being wrong in your timing decisions, running out of money, or losing your long-term capital is still—and has always been—a long-term diversified investment strategy. You can have your own opinion, but the facts are the facts.

So in the end, you choose poverty or prosperity based on how you invest. It's true that you might not be poor if you don't invest in the market, but history shows that there is little else you can do with your money that gives the same returns or rewards—and keeps up with inflation.

I hope you, as both an advisor and an investor, can see that you won't find that truth in today's doomsday headlines, nor in your recent investment idea gone bad, nor any other fear-monger-based opinion. You will find truth in the fact mankind has—and will—continue to create wealth through its effort to improve itself.

Since perception *is* your reality, though, I wrote this book to help you determine how real your reality is or isn't. If you don't agree with these facts, you are certainly entitled to your opinion, but I am not writing this book to prove the facts. The facts actually prove themselves. If your opinion is to disagree with historical facts, then put this book down, because what I have to offer won't help you. If, however, you might be willing to see how the financial industry, the sensationalist media, and the emotions of our clients have been conspiring to cause those clients to miss the rewards that come from the truth of these facts, then keep reading.

We are going to change lives together—starting with your own.

PART YOU:

The Advisor

....

Never trade what you want at the moment for what you want the most.

– John C. Maxwell

The first step toward valuing *them* (your clients) is knowing *you*. You are the only person around who is responsible for you, so it's important to take some time to examine and nurture your best self. It boggles my mind how many financial advisors have no clue who they are, what they want, or what they believe. Therefore, they become people who want what others want, believe what others believe and are controlled by other people's impressions of them. Like the great line from the country song by Aaron Tippin and Buddy Brock, "You've got to stand for something or you'll fall for anything." This section is about you.

So who are you? Until you figure out the answer, you will not reach your full potential. It is a process and requires discipline, inquiry and time. If you haven't taken the time to explore these questions, book a getaway now. Have fun, and make it your goal to be transparent and real with yourself.

Almost everyone has heard of Microsoft's founder, Bill Gates. What most people don't know is that Bill Gates, over the years, has locked himself away in a cottage to reflect on who he is and what he is trying to accomplish. Mr. Gates eats cold pizza and drinks Orange Crush and spends up to a week writing letters to himself…letters that over the years he rereads, reflects on and acts on. Much of what Microsoft has become can be attributed to a man who spent time alone with his thoughts.

Sounds crazy, but it might work, as productivity seminar leader Bob Dunwoody told me many times. Three years into my career, I set aside nine days at a condo in Vail wrestling with these questions. I skied by day and reflected by night. Much of who I am today I attribute to the amount of time I spent trying to find myself. Finding yourself is not a destination; it is an ongoing journey of self-exploration. It is time to start our journey into the *you* inside of *you*. Are you ready?

Find You Inside of You

A chameleon changes shades of color depending on his surroundings, but a chameleon does this to hide. When you don't know who you are, you're likely to be multiple people to multiple people. You change who you are based on your surroundings, and there's a fundamental seed for unhappiness in trying to be all things to all people.

I learned a very painful lesson in college when I was set on accomplishing everything there was to accomplish. I achieved the distinction of being an ambassador to my university. That meant I was one of the guys who wore a jacket in the colors of the alma mater, and got to hobnob with the alumni of the university, the governors of the state, the Board of Education, etc. It was quite the Who's Who crowd to hang with. The only problem was, it also came with having to do some grunt work, like taking a bunch of high school 18-year-old punks on tours of the school in 90 plus degree Florida weather wearing slacks and a jacket. And I thought, *I'm too good to do that. I'm better at hobnobbing.* Besides, I had all these other things I was responsible for, yet I really didn't know what my priority commitments were. I was trying to be all things to all people, because I really hadn't figured out who I was and what I was passionate about—what my commitments were; I didn't care. I thought I could do it all. When you're trying to be all things to all people, however, you get pulled in all directions. That led me to a life-changing meeting and the best lesson I ever had.

After being warned plenty of times, the director of the Alumni Association for the university called me in and sat me down. "Tyson," she said, "In our Friday meeting in two days, you're going to stand up and resign and state that you don't have the time nor the commitment level to be what an ambassador really is. You're not doing the real work that an ambassador is supposed to do, which is to help bring students to this university and give them a reason to come here. All you want to do is hobnob with people, and the quality of your commitment is just not there. Either you're going to stand up and resign and tell the others you are not fulfilling your commitment to be an ambassador, or I'm going to stand up and fire you for not having the commitment to be an ambassador." Then she said this, "You need to realize that you can be great at something, or good at a lot of things. Your choice. And it's all based on the things to which you are committed."

I had to stand up and resign in front of all my peers rather than be fired, and I realized a very valuable lesson: I would, in the future, make sure that instead of getting really good at a lot of things, I would be great at a few things. I still had some serious choices to make, but this was one of the best lessons of my college career. Funny, it didn't come in a classroom or a textbook.

Your Circumstances and Your Stuff Are Not You[1]

To figure out who you are, you must first figure out who you are not. When most people ask you who you are, you answer based on one or both of these two paradigms : Your circumstances or your stuff.

We live in a society that teaches us that who we are is our stuff. This line of thinking says that if you want to be successful, you have to own a Rolex watch. You don't own a Rolex so you must not be a success. Therefore, we get

---

1 Bob Dunwoody (http://www.bob@bobdunwoody.com)

up every morning to do what is necessary to acquire a very fine watch. And what changes?

Nothing.

Now that you bought the watch you need the car. You bought the wrong thing. So we get busy for another two or three years and finally we accumulate a wonderful car and what changes?

Nothing.

Oh, you bought the watch and the car, but it was the house; you should have bought the house, and you bought the wrong thing. What society teaches us we need is driven by a very talented group of people that comprise the advertising industry, on which American business spends billions of dollars trying to make us believe we are our stuff.

Stop! Stop buying stuff thinking you are somehow improving who you are. You are *not* your stuff, especially if most of your stuff is bought with money you don't have and takes away from money you could have.

We also tend to answer the question "Who are you?" by describing our circumstances. For instance, you are your age. You are the college you went to (or didn't go to). You are your father and mother's son or daughter. When I'm engaged in a get-acquainted conversation, you might hear me say: "I'm a financial advisor who has $2 million dollars of production, $200 million in assets under management, five people on my team, a wife named Jenny, three sons, Austin, Nelson and Carson. I have a nice house. I have three cars. I have a 120-acre hunting cabin." In this example, however, I have responded by describing my circumstances and my stuff, not who I really am.

This is profound, because all my circumstances and stuff can change. So now I know who I'm *not*. The core of who I am is *not* my circumstances and not my stuff. Who I really am is immutable. Tyson Ray is someone who helps other people help themselves—hence this book.

I've noticed that when you don't know who you are, by default you identify yourself by circumstances and stuff, which can then control you instead of you controlling yourself. When you become controlled by circumstances and stuff, you are playing the game of "more stuff" instead of engaging in the game of life. Stuff is the powerful thing in the American dream. The desire to acquire is deeply embedded in our social and societal roots. In and of itself, it's not a bad thing, but we must not let it define who we are.

Understanding the core of who you are may seem like a daunting task. Instead of gritting your teeth and sitting down to try and figure it out, just acknowledge the challenge, look at it for a bit, and let some time pass. An amazing phenomenon occurs: the answer will come to you. The first time I asked myself, "Who am I? Who is Tyson Ray really?" I spent an enormous amount of time identifying myself through circumstances, but deep down I knew I was missing something. I realized I had spent the first 30 years of my life not really knowing who I was. The answer seemed to elude me, so I allowed some time to pass as I struggled to find answers to other questions.

I decided to approach the question, "Who am I?" through reflecting on who I want to be. As I stated in the Preface, sometimes it's helpful to start at the end.

So I sometimes imagine I've just died. At my funeral, people are going to reveal who I am today. I decided rather than waiting, I might start now helping write my eulogy. In fact, every now and then I write out what I *hope* will be said so I can focus on making life choices that will ensure I am remembered the way I want.

> *Tyson Ray. Born 1975. Died 20?? after a life of service that impacted our world. He loved the Lord Jesus Christ and served His Lord with all his heart, mind, soul and strength. He did so without judging others who didn't share his beliefs. Tyson was married to Jenny for his whole life. "Tyson was everything I ever wanted in a husband and father of my three sons," Jenny said. Nelson, Austin and Carson said of their father, "Our Dad was a real man; he was our role model and was responsible for helping us know what it looks like to be a real follower of Jesus. He was our encourager to graduate*

from college and our mentor to help us create and succeed with our own families and careers."

Tyson Ray spent much of his time and money giving back to the poorest of poor in this world. In fact Tyson often was heard saying, "The best gift is given to someone who has no way to repay you. It is easy to give and expect something in return, but so much more rewarding to give and expect nothing." By feeding thousands of starving children, building schools, and getting orphans placed into families, Tyson poured his life into helping those who were much less fortunate have something better.

Tyson Ray also impacted thousands of people through his financial advisory career. Not only were the lives of his clients and their families changed for the better from his counsel, but he also helped thousands of financial advisors learn how to positively impact the lives of their own clients. Tyson's life was a compounding effect of positive changes for our world.

Though we have lost Tyson's life, his work continues on in all those he touched with his love!

This makes me want to stop writing this book and go live it! You've got to stop and go write your own. I might not be able to pull it all off, but it is really worth trying. Do you see what can happen? When you start with the end in mind and really think what you want the end to look like, a vision suddenly shows up.

"To Be or Not to Be:" From Vision to Reality

My eulogy above creates a very clear vision of who I am trying hard to be. A vision is not just a picture. A vision is a picture with feeling. The hard part is turning a vision into words and action. Upon reflecting on that vision, I realized quickly I was not being or doing what was necessary for that vision to become true. And that conflict is where our life path is decided.

You see I have to be honest with myself about the choices I must make. I must either start living each day in light of that eulogy—living each day being the *me* that I want to be—or I need to rewrite the eulogy and rethink the vision.

Then I reflected on the truth of where I was spending my time. Author Annie Dillard once said wisely, "How we spend our days is how we live our lives." We need to discover for ourselves how to live this day to impact the rest of our days. If I am committed to a vision of the man I want to be, then I might need to stop being committed to those things I *don't* want to be. Are you being held back because you don't realize you can be anything you want to be? I found myself committed to learning—learning not just how to help people, but how people wanted to be helped.

Once I could see, in my mind's eye, the vision of who I wanted to be, a miraculous thing happened. I rose out of bed each morning infused with a new found energy. I woke each day seeking to help people help themselves and enjoyed the different opportunities by which I was able to do that.

Why do *you* get out of bed in the morning?

When I figured out who I was, it helped me figure out what I am trying to accomplish. I want to help the most people possible say, "Tyson helped me make a difference." Ironically this goal isn't about me. It is about what I can do for others.

What are *you* trying to accomplish?

Most people don't get to live in the paradigm of achieving what they want to accomplish, because they live in the paradigm that they "have" to be doing something. Psychoanalyst Karen Horney called this "The Tyranny of Shoulds." Most people resist "having" to do something, so they do nothing or something different that takes them away from their deepest desires rather than towards them. The trick is to flip this paradigm around. Instead of concentrating on who you think you *have* to be, why not concentrate on being who you *want* to be?

Fingers, Eyeballs and Snowflakes: Dare to be Different

Part of your resistance to thinking too deeply about who you really are is because you are afraid to be different. People are inherently afraid to stand out. The herd mentality to conform is very strong. It is amazing to me, however, how quickly we forget what fingers, eyeballs and snowflakes have in common—not one of them is alike. They are all unique.

If you think about it, individual beauty is a gift to most natural life forms. Each blossom, tree, insect, animal, and ocean wave is formed uniquely. We were created to appreciate our differences, not judge them. However, most human beings feel there is safety in numbers. If everyone is doing it, everyone must be right. There may be some evolutionary advantage to that behavior in the face of a common threat, but how damaging is that philosophy in investing?

If you position yourself as the best performer, your clients are always going to jump ship for the next best performer. Moreover, top performance is unpredictable at best. According to several recent studies, top performing money managers underperform 70% of the time.

Dare to be Different
My favorite shoe. Photo courtesy Crocs™

What a "Croc"!

Instead, position yourself as different, i.e. special. Clients want someone who is willing to stand out from the crowd. Inspiration on this topic came in an unusual form—from Crocs™ (those multi-colored rubber clogs with heel straps). In 2005, while training for an Ironman triathlon, I purchased a pair of unique bright red Crocs™. I wanted something that stood out after jumping out of the water. The Crocs™ embodied everything I always wanted in a shoe—comfortable, indestructible, and easy to clean. My wife made fun of me every time I wore them in public. I didn't care. I loved my Crocs™ when Crocs™ lovers were still a select, discerning few. I remember being in the airport in Alaska and spotted a woman wearing the exact same pair. We immediately bonded. Who else is brave enough to wear such eye-catching, practical, monstrosities? We valued our Crocs™, and we didn't care what the rest of the world thought. And you know what? Because enough people like us decided they valued Crocs™ too, the brand exploded in popularity and is now a household name.

My Crocs™ taught me you sometimes have to accept being odd in the short term to be right in the long term. Moreover, if you know why you are doing what you are doing, you can tolerate standing out.

So who are you? Who you are has everything to do with advising, because it will determine who your ideal client is and who you can help the most.

Who Are You? (An Exercise)

In the space below on the next page, write out your eulogy. Don't think about just who you are now, but what you want to hear about yourself when your life is over. Now let this be a living draft; I suggest you rewrite it annually. Over a few years of doing this for myself, the content changes less and less, because I have found the me I want to be and—more importantly—the me I am committed to being, each and every day.

My Eulogy

Date written _____

What Do You Want?

Thought Precedes Action

– Heinrich Heine based on the philosophy of Aristotle

The problem is not that we aren't working hard enough; it's that we don't know where we're going.

One of the most difficult questions to answer is, "What do you want?" If you can't answer what you want, it will be difficult to guide your clients to get what they want. There is an interesting dynamic that exists in our business: as you help clients accomplish their goals, you can accomplish yours too. The question is, do you know what your goals are?

First, I'd like to clarify something I said earlier. I'm not advocating that you should want "more." I'm simply saying if you don't know what you want, you can easily fall into the game of "more," and it's a game you can't win. It's kind of a default position that happens when you aren't in alignment with who you are or what you truly want. It is easy to get caught up in thinking that what you want is what the herd dictates you should want.

The "more" I'm talking about wanting here comes from an inner place. It's an "essence" want or a "core" want. This type of want is born from authentic desire, not peer pressures, social stigmas or past pain.

Once you know what you want, pursue what you want as if it already is. Pursue it as though your life depended on it, because it does.

Redefining Success

Coming to terms with your core desire may redefine what success looks like to you. In fact, it almost surely will. I'm still astonished how many people enter my office and don't know what they want or what success looks like to them. They sit down and say, "I want to retire." That is the end goal in many a client's mind. "That is great," I say, "but what do you want to do when you retire?" Often I find they don't know what they want to do when they retire. You see for most of their lives, clients have been working with the goal of not working. They called not working retirement. Once they stop working and retire, however, they find out their life is actually doing nothing. They were so focused on working to retire, they didn't have a life and now they are retired and not working and still don't have a life. You can't let someone retire until you know what they will do in their retirement. The best questions are, "Who will you be when you do not need to work?" "When you are retired, what will make you want to get out of bed?"

I had a midlife crisis at 30. In my early twenties, success meant becoming a million dollar producer by the age of 30. I wrote down, "I will be a million dollar producer before I am 30," and I tracked it. At the age of 29, I did become a million dollar producer, but then I realized true success was not a production number.

This is when I began to realize I didn't know what I wanted. I was clear about who I was, but I was still focusing on the wrong path and finish line.

The moment of truth arrived in 2008 while bouncing Keily on my knee. Keily was the adopted daughter of my brother-in-law and his wife, both pastors. She was the newborn child of an inner city woman who already had five children. Being unable to have children themselves, my brother-in-law and his wife qualified because of Keily's mother's specific request that the adopted parents be pastors, but they lacked the $20,000 needed to execute the adoption. That's where I was able to help, so within 24 hours they brought Keily into their home and family. I realized that by having money, I was able to change Keily's life and the lives of my sister and brother in-law forever. My paradigm for success instantly changed.

From that moment forward, why I do what I do changed. I don't work for money anymore. In fact, I don't work anymore. Living out a passion is not work, it is living. I live to make a difference for people. I live to help children like Keily, and this passion has allowed me to do humanitarian work for some of the poorest children on our planet, like those in Haiti. I work for the families of my clients and for the community. I define my success by the lives I touch, not the money I make, and my work has taken on a whole new meaning. I work with clients to help them. I take the money I make from helping them to improve their lives and help even more people improve their lives.

Changing Why We Work

It starts with a decision in your mind. Your business is random in the sense that there is no specific pattern or path to follow ...no "seven steps to success," if you will. You can succeed in endless ways. Success itself, however, is not random. Success is created in specific ways, and most people don't understand this.

Often in our world, and specifically in our industry, what we want is tied to some kind of financial income. How much you want to make might be a question you need to answer before you can know what you want.

At some point compensation is part of who you are or, better put, derived by who you are. It is also something people seek to achieve. What I have discovered is once you have enough money that you no longer live just for making money, two things happen. First, you are likely to make even more money, and then you have much more fun in the process. To get there, however, you need to get yourself out of survival mode or at least figure out how much you feel you need so you can become unconscious about your own money. They say time is money, so if we figure out how much time you spend working, you should figure out how much your time is worth. Here's how to approach the question, "How much money do you want to make?"

Let's say you've looked at your expenses, added some savings and some vacation emergency money, and you decide you want a monthly average net paycheck of $20,000.

To achieve this, you need a gross paycheck around $33,000 a month if you figure 40% total taxes and withholdings. That would mean you need an annual gross income of $400,000 ($33,000 times 12 months). If you assume a 40% payout, then you need a gross production of $1,000,000 (multiplied by 40%) to earn $400,000.

If you are a fee-based advisor, at 1% you need $100,000,000 of assets under management; at 1.25% you need $80,000,000; and at 1.5% fee you only need around $66,600,000. Using this formula, then, you can easily figure out how many assets under management you need in order to achieve the income you want to make. I will come back to this later.

There is a danger in not knowing what you want. America tells us "You can have it all!" I agree; however, I'm painfully aware that most people never get it "all," because most people focus too much on "all" the world has to offer rather on the "it" which they really want from the "all." The trick to life is to find out what "it" is. People often misunderstand what "having it all" really means. "It" is not everything. "It" is something. "It" is specifically something to which you are committed. There is a difference between what you want and what you are committed to. If you want to be a financial advisor, and yet you keep making individual stock recommendations for a commission without a plan, in my opinion, you are not committed to being a financial advisor. If you want to be thinner and keep eating in excess and not exercising, you are not committed to being thin.

Forgive me for being enormously simple. I know it's not that easy, but it's important to get your mind around this so you'll understand what comes next.

At 30,000 feet, sitting in our seats on our flight to our honeymoon, my wife Jenny and I realized we had a problem. I had created the problem myself when I handed my new bride a blank legal pad and said, "Please write out your life's mission statement, your 3-year, 5-year, lifetime goals, and your definition of a successful husband. Oh, and while you're at it, include your definition of a successful father." I went on to explain I would redo my own answers to these questions and then in about two hours we would compare our individual mission, goals and definitions in order to create our own as a couple. I will never forget Jenny's response, "You have got to be kidding!"

I found we had a problem in how we think about the future. I liked to plan out into the future, to dream and set goals. Jenny preferred to wake up and decide what she was going to do today. Whereas I thought in terms of months and years into the future. Jenny thought about today and maybe tomorrow.

So, I changed my request to ask her to make me a list. The rules for the list were: 1) Assume that anything in life is possible; 2) If you could do anything in life without limitation, write on the list what it would be; 3) You can write as many as things as you want, but you have to come up with as least 10 things. (In my relationship with Jenny it works better to say, "I bet you can't come up with 10 things.")

Her list taught me a lot about who she was. Remember, I had already married the woman, so you'd think I would already have known her pretty well. A few items on her list:

1. Paint the kitchen red
2. Cure Multiple Sclerosis (her brother-in-law has the disease)
3. Learn sign language
4. Read Bible daily and get into a Bible study
5. Buy new clothes in New York
6. Pay off the mortgage

Once she was done with the list of about 12 things, I made my next request: Please highlight the items on the list to which you are committed.

This was amazing. Jenny only had about six things to which she was committed. I kept her list and gave her mine, and then for the next 12 months we were able to encourage each other to accomplish the goals on our lists.

I learned a great deal from doing this with my wife. I remember during one summer, I had a great month in production. We had a little extra money in the bank, and I had accomplished most everything on my list. I then looked at Jenny's list. I noticed one highlighted item she was committed to making happen, "Paint the kitchen red." Now please understand, I could care less the color of the walls in my kitchen. I was concentrating on goals to change the world. I was committed to millions of dollars in new assets, new production and increased revenues. I was thinking, "Who has time to be painting kitchen walls, and furthermore, who cares?" If I had said this out loud, it would have been the biggest mistake I ever made, because my wife's desire to paint the kitchen red (her "it") was just as important as my desire to build more relationships (my "it"). I called her and said, "We've got the money to paint the kitchen, so why don't you go ahead and make it happen."

I learned two important lessons:

1. Involve your spouse in identifying what you want together.
2. Quit thinking the list is too long. Take time to make it; then develop priorities based on where you feel committed.

We do this exercise each year. Each year I learn my own list changes a little and so does Jenny's. However, knowing each other's list and helping each other accomplish our "It List" has been a huge benefit to our marriage.

What's on your "It List?"

Take 10 minutes and write down what you would want if you could have it all. It won't even take you 10 minutes. I'll bet you won't have more than 10-12 things. Remember if you could do anything with no restrictions—if all things were possible—what would they be?

Item	"It List"	Committed
1.		
2.		
3.		
4.		
5.		
6.		
7.		
8.		
9.		
10.		

11.

12.

Now mark the things on the list to which you are committed. What would you be willing to work for, sacrifice and make happen?

What you will learn is you are only committed to three to five things, and you'll realize you are currently spending a lot of time, energy and money on things to which you are not committed. If you have a relationship with someone else, have him or her create their list and share your lists together.

Take Responsibility

Successful people fiercely believe responsibility equals freedom. Take 100% responsibility for yourself and your life. "If it's meant to be it's up to me!" Take 100% responsibility and expect nothing from anyone. Identify those things—and those things only—to which you are committed and then be responsible for those things. An erroneous belief system has taught us that responsibility is a burden and should be avoided.

For example, I am committed to being married. This means I give 100% and expect nothing in return. We learned and wrongly believe that marriage should be 50/50. I believe divorce lawyers would be out of business if every married person were committed to giving 100% to their marriage.

What About Your Time?

How much time do you have? Do you ever walk out of your office and say, "What did I do today?" We spend a lot of time doing what we shouldn't be doing. Start spending time on what is important and minimizing time spent on things that aren't important.

According to the Cerulli Advisor Time Allocation Survey, financial advisors spend 18% of their time on client acquisition, 29.4% of their time in client meetings and 52.6% of their time doing other activities. Other activities include service, managing managers, research, asset management, administration, operations, training and compliance. The process outlined in this book will help allow you to reduce time spent on other activities and maximize time spent with clients, which is the most important aspect of our business.

How much time do you want to work? Most of our time is spent reacting to circumstances and client demands that are coming at us. I found that if I make just four proactive phone calls or appointments a day, that is enough to grow and sustain a business. I am astonished how hard it is to just do the two proactive calls in morning and two in the afternoon. I'm further astonished at how few people actually practice this. The secret is you have to schedule it and make sure you provide margin in your schedule to react to other items that may or may not have been completed during the week.

That is why I only schedule work four days a week. I schedule Fridays free. Not Fridays off—Fridays flexible so I have time to catch up on all the stuff piled up from the week that did not get done.

I took the concept further and decided not only to schedule Fridays free but the fourth week of each month free too for what I call margin time. Why do I do this? You might think it doesn't make sense, but given the fact that our business is one built on interruptions, I think it makes complete sense to allow time for them. If you are so busy chasing too many rabbits, you will be burned out and start losing clients. Build time into your schedule to allow for the unexpected.

The concept of starting with the end in mind doesn't have to just be applied to your whole life. You can start with just a week from today. Think out 7 days and look back. Now ask yourself, what you would need to do to control how you spend your time so that 7 days from now you could look back with no regrets. Now what about a month out or a year out? The farther out you go, the more general the use of time becomes, but it starts you on a path of controlling your time. Once you become committed to being who you are, controlling your time allows you to do the things necessary to be yourself and have the things you want to have.

Map out your time for a normal week. Better yet map out how you want your time to look. Every few months I will change this simple little Excel spreadsheet, but I will create an ideal week. If I control my time, it's how I would like my week to look. Here's the amazing thing: what I sketch out often becomes what happens. I also found that if I don't write down anything, the only thing I don't have is enough time.

Process Driven Schedule:

Time	Monday	Tuesday	Wednesday	Thursday	Friday	Saturday	Sunday
5:00 AM	READ	READ		READ	READ		
6:00 AM	CARSON	CARSON	BREAKFAST WITH SCOTT	CARSON	CARSON	FAMILY TIME	FAMILY TIME
6:30 AM	WAKE UP KIDS	WAKE UP KIDS		WAKE UP KIDS	WAKE UP KIDS		
7:00 AM	PLAN DAY	PLAN DAY		PLAN DAY	PLAN DAY		
8:30 AM	WORK OUT	WORK OUT	APPT	WORK OUT	WORK OUT		
10:30 AM	APPT	APPT	APPT	APPT		CATCH UP	
12:00 PM	RETURN CALLS	RETURN CALLS	RETURN CALLS	RETURN CALLS		CATCH UP	
12:30 PM	LUNCH	LUNCH	LUNCH	LUNCH			
1:00 PM	NAP	NAP	NAP	NAP	MARGIN		
1:30 PM	APPT	APPT	APPT	APPT		MARGIN	MARGIN
3:00 PM	RETURN CALLS	RETURN CALLS	RETURN CALLS	RETURN CALLS			
3:30 PM	APPT	APPT		APPT			
5:00 PM	RETURN CALLS	RETURN CALLS	FAMILY TIME	RETURN CALLS			
5:30 PM	APPT	APPT		APPT	PICK UP KIDS	CHURCH	
7:00 PM	CATCH UP	CATCH UP	CHURCH	CATCH UP			
8:00 PM	FAMILY TIME	FAMILY TIME		FAMILY TIME	FAMILY TIME		PLAN WEEK

I also involve Jenny in helping me decide what should be on the schedule. Where does family time fit in the best? When should I put in my time to work out or plan for the future? One great part of this tool is sharing future expectations of my time with my wife. Because Jenny helped me create this list, she knows I will be home in the mornings to help with the kids, but then three nights a week I will not be home until 8pm. Jenny doesn't have to worry or start questioning where I have been when I come home late on a Tuesday night, because the schedule on the fridge at home shows that Tyson works till 8pm on Mondays, Tuesdays and Thursdays.

I even schedule a nap every day in my office. In Outlook, I can create a recurring to-do list. I hand out the schedule once a quarter to everyone in my office who needs access to it. I realize not everyone has an assistant, but most of you have a receptionist. If someone is calling in to get an appointment, just put them in an available slot and set aside the time. I don't believe you should get into the habit of letting clients come in and see you whenever they want.

Much has been written about time management, and much of it is useful. I just wanted to share the system by which I manage my time as a successful financial advisor. This is a suggestion only; it works for my office and me. You have to create a schedule and thought process around time that works for you. Remember, when considering time spent, think first about who you are, what you are trying to accomplish and what your clients are trying to accomplish. This will guide your experience with time.

By building a weekly schedule, you are now able to control when you meet with clients. It allows you to function more like other professionals. Go call your dentist and ask for any appointment. They will say Monday at 10:30 or Tuesday at 1:30pm. When you are scheduling appointments for your clients, rather than giving the impression that you are just wide open and can meet whenever, give them a specific point in time, and let them decide what works best. It's tempting to give clients the impression they can meet with you whenever, because when you started in the business, you could. As your business grows, however, it can become a problem if clients think they can just come see you whenever they want. Control the problem before it starts by setting when you will have appointments before you have them.

There is another reason for creating a system for setting appointments. If you ask a potential client to just come and meet with you in your office, the person is going to focus on whether or not they want to meet with you at all. Instead, ask them if they can come see you at 3pm Monday or Thursday at 10:30. What I have found is the person's mind shifts to their schedule. Rather than focusing on deciding if they want to meet with you, they are focusing their thoughts around their schedule and when they are free. I have had people come in for an initial meeting and say, "Okay, why am I here?"

Protecting Your Most Precious Asset: You

Balance: The problem with this job is that your work is never done. Your responsibilities are endless. This job can suck the life out of you. If you're not careful, this job can change you. You've got to protect yourself. Are you losing yourself in your job? Balance is critical, and you are responsible for yourself first! Finding out what you really want may require realizing you have been taught some wrong belief systems.

I believe a balanced life should include four different areas: God, family, work and you. Your belief system on balance might call for pleasing God, your family and your career, but what about yourself? I believe, God loves you and made you who you are, so you are valuable and worth preserving. Seek Him and ask, "Who do you want me to be?" Listen for an answer and act when you hear it.

Figuring out how to balance work and family can be a real struggle, but here is an important warning: Your spouse married you for you, the person you were when he/she fell in love with you. Your manager hired you before you had your current job. In both cases they brought you into their lives when you were an earlier version of yourself. Responsibilities and expectations from both family and work can be unhealthy and can change you into someone your family, your clients, your manager or you yourself may not like as much.

For example, I want to be a good father, so I need to play with my son. If I base my success of being a good father on how much my son wants to play, I will have a problem, because my five-year-old son will never say, "Okay, Dad, today we have played enough." It is never enough. It's the same with work. There is always one more call, one more form to have signed, one more follow-up to make. You are never done. Work can drain you until you're no longer your best self. Left unchecked, you change from the person your family fell in love with. You become a different you than the one who had time for God. You become a different you whose joy and peace are robbed by the pressure of an unbalanced life. Take care of yourself. You are the only one responsible for making sure you have "you time."

How do you recharge? How do you reward yourself? What do you enjoy doing by yourself that has nothing to do with church, family and work? Are you doing it? If you lose too much of who you are in trying to meet the expectations of what others want you to be, you end up being different from what they wanted to start out with. This leads you do to things that are out of character, hurtful to yourself and others, and which you never intended. People don't set out to have a midlife crisis, divorce or addiction. They simply lost the balancing act by forgetting they needed to make sure they were responsible to themselves as well as to others.

Invest in Yourself: You make an impact when you invest in yourself, because as CEO of your own life, you're strengthening your most valuable asset. Here is a crazy concept, but it's true: In order to do more for others, you may have to do more for yourself. Nurture your body and your mind by investing in your personal fitness, health and learning. Never accept status quo; always strive for the next level.

I realized I had to invest my own capital back into my business as any good owner would do. That is one heck of a snowflake idea. We are in an industry where every wholesaler wants to give us or sell us something in exchange for dollars, referrals, or something else. I just chose to invest in me. I buy quality promotional materials that reflect who I am and what I do in a classy way. I pay for continuing education (e.g., seminars, courses, webinars) so I can stay on top of what's going on in my industry. I invest in books and tapes to feed my mind and make me more valuable to my clients. For every $100 dollars I make, I give $10 away to charity and I invest $10 back into my business. You have to invest in you. Too many people look to others to invest in them without investing in themselves first.

Investing in your business might take the form of investing in your clients. It can sure cement a client relationship when you send them flowers and a bottle of wine on their 50th anniversary. That's a $50 investment in your business too.

I knew this from a very young age. Although I would not advise to anyone to do this, I went $16,000 in credit card debt at the age of 23 because I knew I had to invest in my business. I hadn't made any money yet in my business. It didn't matter though, because I was totally committed.

Are you investing in you?

Give it Away: When you figure out who you are and what you want, you figure out the game of life isn't about you. It is about the privilege of being able to give back. Don't do like so many others and waste many years before you realize life is about giving back to others.

It was my last semester of college, and despite saving $100 a month in two mutual funds, I was completely broke. I was beginning to discover that life was not taking for myself as much as giving to others. However with only $40 in my checking account, I didn't have much to give anyone, and with only two months left until college graduation, I still had no job offers on the table. Sitting in church realizing my fate, I made a pact with God. I was going to donate 10% of everything I made back to doing something good. So I wrote a check for $4 and that was that.

After college, I got a job at a regional brokerage firm to broker financial products to clients. At that time getting a job at a 117-year-old financial firm right out of college was unheard of. After having a small monthly salary, my compensation transitioned completely to commissions. Each month I would start at zero and had no idea what my month-to-month income would me. After six months in the business, I received my first check for $400. I had been working half days (12 hour shifts) five days a week and usually a good part of Saturdays, with little to no reward. I remember when my boss handed me that first check, he stated with a smirk, "Looks like it is going to be beanies and weenies for you this month." $400 dollars was not enough to make my rent or cover my car payment, and couldn't even make the minimum payment on my credit card.

This was poverty or worse, as I was taking out money on new credit cards to make my payments (something you should never do). I reached a point where I had to make a decision. Was I committed to this career where I could impact people for better? Was I committed to being a different kind of broker (at the time, the title financial advisor didn't exist)?

I was eating tuna, baked beans and apple juice. Why? Because it was what I could buy the most of with my $20 a week grocery allowance. I was getting used to a Spartan diet and virtually no furniture in my apartment. The bed was on the floor; the TV was on the floor. I had pictures hung on the walls, but coming home to no chair to sit in and no table to eat on was a consistent reminder I was failing. Yet the more my circumstances reflected failure, the more committed I became to succeeding.

Despite my austere living circumstances, I kept my promise to God and wrote a $40 check and gave it away. Exactly six months from the date of my first $400 check, I received my first $4,000 check for the month and was able to give away $400. Exactly six months from that date, I received my first $40,000 check and was able to write a $4,000 check.

Why do I give back? At the ripe age of 22, I found myself miserable. From the outside I looked perfectly content, but I hated myself. I hated the fact that I was so consumed with gaining power and position that I didn't care who I stepped on to achieve my goals. But, I read the right book, and realized that giving back was the right thing to do--with no expectation of return.

Ditching the expectation is an important part of happy giving. People get upset if their expectations are not met. The best way to go through life is to expect nothing! When you don't have any expectations, you'll never be upset. Don't expect anything from anyone and you'll be surprised what comes back to you.

I believe this giving path is the path to freedom. It comes when you can give and expect nothing in return. Giving to others who are not able to help themselves stirs something deep within you. It brings a feeling of joy and satisfaction no money can buy. The problem is you have to do it to experience it. Give it a try and see how it feels. I suggest giving to something specific— not some general fund, but a specific cause that inspires you.

Do you give back?

Reward Yourself: Do you reward yourself? Once you know who you are and what you want—once you are giving back to the rest of the world and doing the things to which you are committed—the only thing left to do is reward yourself. Way to go! Good job! As you find yourself accomplishing what you said you'd do, assign rewards to those things. Too often, we operate under the false belief system that we must punish ourselves when something is not done well or a goal is not achieved. The job environment offers plenty of free punishment for everyone.

Successful people reward themselves. Don't confuse rewards with money. Self-rewards can be as simple as saying "I like myself." Going for a massage, or taking a trip can be powerful rewards. And, it's fun to discover that the more I reward myself, the more I reward others. The whole game is contagious!

Why no try rewarding yourself ? No one cares more than you do.

PART VALUE:

The Practice

....

It is my observation most people get ahead in the time that others waste.

– Henry Ford

Most financial advisors are not allowed the opportunity to define their value or understand what kind of practice they are going to have. They are taught how to pass the exams needed to get licensed, trained on the systems and products of the firm for which they get their paycheck, and then they're thrown out into the world to gather clients and assets. In order to prove their worth and fend off personal poverty, the brand new financial advisor is tempted to take anyone on as a client for any reason. Only an estimated one in five new financial advisors will make it five years, so firms place big demands on a newbie for new assets, new accounts and production. It's a race for survival.

No financial advisor who makes it has any desire to ever go back and start over. After 200 or 300 clients acquired at random, however, the financial advisor is left with a practice, business and value has become the least common denominator. In order for financial advisors to impact the world, they need to start over. The good news is, you can, without having to give up all your clients to do it.

You are running a business. As in any business, you need to create a business plan and define a few things. Starting with a blank sheet of paper, you need to define what kind of business you want, what kinds of clients you want, and what kind of value you are going to provide.

This whole section is about starting over without having to start from scratch. You already have the clients, but you no longer have to allow them to decide what kind of business you are going to have. Rather than letting external circumstances and clients define your value or your practice (which will always end up as the lowest common denominator), why not define it yourself based on the highest common denominator? This is not only best for you, it's best for your client as well. In order for financial advisors to build what I feel is the highest value-add business for the future, they need to start over. To begin, let's start over with what we think about a few things.

Stop predicting the future. You're not any good at it. Since no one else is any good at it either, there is no value in trying to pretend you are.

Stop Predicting the Future

According to Nick Murray, 2007 recipient of the Malcolm S. Forbes Public Awareness Award for Excellence in Advancing Financial Understanding, there are three things no one can predict or control:

1. The economy
2. Markets
3. Future Investment Performance[1]

If that is true, and I believe it is, then it is also true that your value added cannot be these things that no one can know or control. This is why as an industry, we have to put disclosures that past does not guarantee the future, because no one knows the future, and you had better not pretend you do.

Yet for most of you in the financial industry, the vast majority of your time is spent talking with clients about your opinion of the direction of the

1 Nick Murray (http://www.nickmurray.com)

economy, markets and which individual investments will be the best place for the future. The world and your clients are trying to suck you into the black abyss of the unknown (and unknowable), yet they're ready to fire back at you when your opinion of the future ends up eventually being wrong. The path to hell begins with that innocent question from the client, "What do you think about (*fill in the blank with a stock or bond name*)?"

Since you are the professional, your client expects you to have an opinion on such things. However the only answer to this line of inquiry that can be right 100% of the time is, "I have no idea." You cannot predict the future. When you start admitting what you can and can't do—when you stop trying to spit back results of all the research you can read (which is really the sum total of everyone else's best guess)—you then can start speaking truth, brutal honest truth. Then you'll be close to understanding one aspect of that wonderful verse from scripture, "The truth shall set you free."

If you can admit to yourself that you can't possibly know or predict the future direction of the economy, markets and future investment performance with any degree of accuracy (which is okay because no one else can either), then you might be on a new path to provide real value to your clients.

In 2002, I stopped trying to figure it out. I now tell clients I can't predict the future. What I have going for me is that no one else knows either. So then what is our job? I feel our job is to change the behavior of our clients through strategic planning and a predetermined investment strategy designed to maximize their chances of having and doing what they need and want in the future.

The Real Role of a Financial Advisor

Advisors who try to make their "value add" involve get-rich insinuations and "I can make you more than the next guy" promises are not advisors; they are brokers/salesmen. They often can't and don't deliver on their sales pitch, but they do make sure they sound good and get paid. There is no long-term value to this model. I know many very good people who are struggling to be the performance-based, hot idea, market-timing, trading, financial-product-peddling salesperson, when they are hard wired to add more value than that.

Speaking about "value" is like saying the word "love". It is a word whose meaning is only as true as the actions that come with it. Do you live to add value? Our advisory business is about value. Plain and simple: value your clients, and add value to their lives. Most people think financial advisors are here to help people make money. The industry tells us the way to make clients money is through better investment selection, market timing, and our own superior expertise. This is a myth. Our job is not to make money, but to be the stewards of the money our clients have already made.

To think you can make someone money is a trap. Clients are happy to set the trap for you. Especially those clients who didn't save enough money 30 years before you ever met them. You see, they want someone to be responsible for their future since they were not responsible for their own future prior to hiring you.

So here is the question: If your job is not to predict the future of the economy, markets or future rates of investment returns and your job is not to make clients money, what *is* your job?

Your primary job is to help clients behave differently.

Clients need their financial advisor to help protect them from themselves through behavior management. Once they become our clients, then we should really become behavior managers. Our job is to teach our clients:

- To behave as people who can't predict the future.
- To behave as people who need to save for their 30 years of retirement.
- To behave as people who plan ahead for how much they can spend, and when they can spend it.
- To behave as people who do not act upon emotion in response to the media, markets, and the herd mentality when making decisions.

We are here to help our clients be different, do different and—as a result—have different.[2]

---

2 Bob Dunwoody (http://www.bob@bobdunwoody.com)

The whole thing is about behavior. At the end of the day, the value you bring to the business is how you behave and what you know about how people behave when it comes to their money. Base your behavior on the facts. My value proposition: I help people do things differently. People make bad decisions with alarming consistency, because too many investment professionals don't understand how to change from selling to advising.

I believe our business should focus on the following areas:

- How to take distributions from lifetime savings
- How to make wealth last as long as possible
- How to make decisions on what and where to spend money
- When to take the money out of investments and when to set money aside

Once you understand your primary role as an advisor is behavior management, the job becomes clear. You will be advising your clients to basically maintain their balance between:

- Needs versus wants
- Risk versus reward
- Long-term goals versus short-term needs
- Present satisfactions versus future regret

The whole process starts with taking the time to have a conversation with the client about what their money is *for*, and this conversation should be ongoing for the rest of that client's life. Even though no one knows or can predict the future of the economy, markets and future investment returns, everyone should be able to tell you what they want or need to spend money on in the next 12-36 months.

Finding out what a client's needs are in the short term (less than 36 months out) can help you plan what funds are needed to meet these short-term obligations and what funds are needed to be set aside for the future needs beyond 36 months. After identifying what short term, annual lifestyle expenses a client has, the advisor gets to move the client towards fulfilling his dreams.

This is where an advisor finds out what the client's lifetime bucket list check-off items are. Go back and take your clients through the "It List" exercise to find out what they dream about versus what they are committed to. In helping clients behave differently, it is to help them understand that rather than being someone who is hired to make them money, you are there to help them spend their money in ways and at a pace that they won't regret later.

Once armed with an understanding of a client's short-term financial needs, long-term lifestyle, annual income needs and the "It List," you are ready to help protect the clients from themselves. You will then be able to help clients set money aside to finance those items, and help clients make decisions regarding spending that avoids future regret. If the advisor is unnecessarily conservative, the client may never get to do something she's always wanted to do, thus creating regret over a lost opportunity. If the advisor lets the client spend too freely, the money could run out before the end of the client's life, creating an entirely different kind of regret.

The ultimate measure of a financial advisor's success is not his compensation; it's sitting down with the client 10, 15, and 20 years down the road, and reflecting back on all of the things the client was able to accomplish with her money. If the advisor has been able to help the client identify and articulate her goals and dreams at the start of their relationship, and then has helped her accomplish all of them within the realm of possibility, then all of a sudden that value added is priceless.

The hardest part for clients to realize is that without someone to advise them on when and how much to take out of their retirement portfolio, they might spend their money more on a whim rather than any kind of plan, focusing more on what they want in the moment instead of what they need for a lifetime. They will likely end up regretting those decisions down the road. This decision process is really a life or death financial process, because to outlive your money—e.g., to run out of money and be unable to even maintain your basic lifestyle—is probably the greatest risk many clients have to face—greater than any market risk or temporary losses in the market. The unchecked consumption and desire to acquire and to accomplish can dramatically compromise the ability of a client's assets to meet ever-increasing expenses of basic living. The reality is poverty stinks for both you and your clients. You can't build a long-term financial practice with clients who are going to run out of money.

So to recap, the risk of giving poor advice on market timing and investment selection may be avoided by not allowing yourself to believe the lie that you can do this in the first place. Your job, instead, is to help the client create a plan for cash flow needs: major purchases and accomplishing things on their lifetime "It List." This plan can let everyone understand what the money is for. Your value is to help the client behave so they can have what they told you they wanted. Then together you get to fight for the future against the secret retirement killer, inflation.

Client (mis)behavior, market timing, and investment selection can all blow your client's wealth up in the short term. In fact, avoiding the mistakes in the short term may help keep your clients from having to worry about the long term. Once you are poor, you are usually poor forever. Since you are going to seek to protect your clients and avoid the short-term damage they can do to their financial future, all that is left is to fight inflation. Your clients don't want to wake up in the morning and admit that their greatest concern is fighting the cancer of inflation, but it is. Yet once a client understands your value is to help them behave better, you can work together to fix inflation. They want their greatest concern to be waking up in the morning and figuring out how they can fund this year's vacation. Heaven forbid they wake up worrying about whether they'll have enough money to live on at the end of their lives.

Ask the Critical Question

In the end--for every person--there is one question that should start the process; the response will lead you to the kind of plan that will best meet the need:

"Do you want to spend your money to the last penny living the best life you can afford, or do you have a specific dollar amount you desire to leave as your financial legacy to people or charity?"

If the latter, then an important follow-up question would be, "Are you willing to make sacrifices in your lifestyle today, and possibly compromise what you can do in your future in order to leave a financial legacy after you are gone?"

Not only are these questions great ways to start the value-of-planning conversation, but they also quickly get to the heart of helping you and your client decide what the end game for their estate plan will look like. With that one decision—whether they want to spend their principal down to nothing or preserve some amount in their estate—you can put in place a pretty sophisticated planning mechanism. Simply make sure you understand the client's income needs in relation to the client's major expenditure expectations.

That is a better conversation for any financial advisor to have with their clients than one focused on what investments they should buy or last week's hot stock. Too many advisors are selling last week's winning lotto numbers— for a fee, or for a charge or for a commission—instead of focusing on what the client wants to do, experience, or buy in their retirement. What is the reward for the client who has been saving his whole life to have some freedom to go and enjoy life? That is the conversation to be having with him.

The reason I am suggesting that an advisor shouldn't have to spend time talking to clients about specific investment assets and market trends is because I believe a properly allocated portfolio, once in place, properly diversified, and properly re-balanced on an automatic basis (which helps remove the client and the advisor from screwing it up) should never be undone—just maintained! Thus once a predetermined investment strategy is in place, an advisor's job actually becomes to help the client do nothing with their portfolio. In my opinion, doing nothing often ends up with the best rewards, because it is the hardest thing to do when the world is screaming at us to react to the ever changing, short-term, dramatic events or the latest hot idea that others think can't fail.

Once properly put in place, I believe the best thing to do is almost always nothing, unless we are setting something aside for the future needs of a client's major purchase. Advisors make a huge mistake when they get so caught-up in deciding what the client should be in, and what they shouldn't be in, and how to re-diversify that they frequently lose focus on how the money should be used in the long-term. All too often, this approach results in exposing their client's portfolio to either A) a permanent short-term risk that could possibly be avoided by diversification, or B) a too-conservative investment strategy in cash or the like that cripples the ability for those assets to keep up with inflated costs and can severely compromise the client's living standard in the future.

Retirees need to hire a lifetime advisor—more than any other professional—to help them know when to take distributions from their wealth throughout the rest of their life. It's not the accumulation of wealth that the advisor can control, but rather making sure that they help the client create a road map (plan) of how and when distributions should be made of the wealth they have worked so hard to accumulate. The financial advisor should work with the client to control this distribution planning—doing so adds value far beyond the current industry norm.

Seeing is not Believing

Not everything is as it seems, so we must be careful when we draw conclusions too quickly that affect our investment decisions. We simply cannot rely on our perceptions, intuitions or gut feelings alone.

It has been clearly shown that investors tend to rely on their perceptions, making the same investing mistakes over and over. Fortunately, studies by some of the leading academics in the field of behavioral finance have shown that investors' irrational behavior tends to be systematic. In other words, virtually everyone reacts the same way when placed in certain situations. This systematic behavior makes it possible to explain why so many people simultaneously make the wrong decision—they are a herd of rational people acting irrationally.

It's just important to keep in mind that investment illusions—your own and those of your clients—must be identified early and counteracted in an appropriate manner.

The stark truth is that investors are typically unable to consistently outperform the market on a risk-adjusted basis. In my opinion the market's efficiency in valuing securities is extremely quick and accurate, and it does not permit investors to find undervalued stocks *on a consistent basis*.

Day-to-day price changes follow a random walk pattern. This pattern occurs because future events can't be predicted from past information since current stock prices reflect currently known information. Therefore, price changes are unpredictable and random. If prices move in a random fashion, any trading rules or techniques will be useless. New information must be unexpected; otherwise it would be reflected in the current stock price.

There is a whole new area of study called Behavioral Finance. I suggest you become a student of this discipline. I recommend reading a book on this topic called *Behavioral Investment Counseling* by Nick Murray, which is available at www.nickmurray.com.

Planning Redefined

When I'm talking about planning, I'm not talking about the 60-page mumbo-jumbo investment proposal with which the industry wants to stuff clients' mailboxes. Planning starts with a relationship between advisor and client. From that relationship, we are afforded the opportunity to identify your specific philosophies around debt, taxation, cash reserves (emergency fund), investment strategy and how that compares with your clients' philosophies, debt, taxation, cash reserves, and investment strategy. A plan, in its simplest terms, is a road map that will guide and transition clients from where they are to where you feel they need to be.

My planning recommendations often flow through the following assumptions:

- The best retirement is a debt-free retirement.
- The sooner a client can become debt-free the sooner a client can accumulate wealth.

- It is risky to borrow money to use for investing, hoping to make returns greater than the interest paid on the loan.
- Years before retirement, the client should think about their debt load.

I recommend a critical order of suggested activities inside a plan:
- All excess cash flow—all investable dollars—should be directed toward paying off all short-term debts with the exception of three things: car payment, house payment or college loans.
- Once a client has no debt beyond those three, tax-advantaged strategies should be the focus by maxing out retirement accounts 401K, IRA, etc. It doesn't make sense to be in a rush to pay down your mortgage before maxing out your 401K.

Many advisors have a hard time recommending or focusing on tax planning strategies, because for many it should start with a 401K, and that's not where an advisor can make much money. To max out $17,000 a year in 2012, or $22,500 a year for those 50 years of age (maximum deferral contribution to 401K), is a lot of money. Consider a married couple over the age of 50 who can reduce an estimated state and federal tax bracket of 25% by putting $45,000 in their 401Ks (assuming they can). Some advisors do not suggest clients do this because most advisors do not control the 401K plan where these funds go. Thus, the advisor does not get paid to make this recommendation, but the brutal truth is unless the advisor can create an annual return to ensure their client recovers from the tax liability they get when they do not max out retirement savings, they are going to reduce the long-term wealth the client could potentially have and increase the annual tax liability for the client.

I have had many clients maxing out their 401k plans that ask me my favorite question, "Is this the right thing to do?" My response is, "Well, unless you want to just pay the IRS extra and pay me for helping you pay more in taxes, it's exactly the right thing to do." Often the best advice to a client—the advice you must give if you're truly looking out for his best interest—may actually be trading your loss for the client's gain. Yes, there may be some short-term negatives in revenue to the advisor, but the client who retires after years of maximizing the tax advantages of retirement plans should have significantly more money in retirement than the client who was told not to max the 401k. Planning is a tool to help clients behave better and understand how recommendations benefit them personally.

Many advisors don't get involved in debt reduction planning, but if my job is to help clients build wealth, I need to make sure they get the guidance they need so they can build enough wealth for me to manage in their retirement.

To be blunt, I want you to sacrifice your own best short-term interest to make sure you're recommending what is in your client's long-term interest. In my own practice, this is non-negotiable, and I consider it an investment in my reputation and peace of mind. If you do not have integrity and ethics, put this book down, because it is not going to mean anything to you.

The Plan versus the Investments

Why is the plan more important than the investments? The reality is there are no special investments. The world's capital markets are available to anyone. The media, society and people in general are exposed everywhere to investment ideas, options and decisions. There's nothing special here. Financial advisors cannot add value by putting their focus on the actual investments. Their focus must be the plan if they expect to add real value to the relationship.

The plan is more important than the investments, because the plan directs the investments. Without the plan, the clients too often allow the investments to direct their decisions. Which is a primary source of behavior issues. When the client has thought through what their money is for and created a plan for that money, many behavior issues can be avoided.

Planning includes estate planning. It is worth noting that the one who advises the client on the estate plan typically wins. The estate plan is designed to cover all the assets and often reveals all the assets. The financial advisor who makes his clients comfortable with having an ongoing conversation on what they want their estate plan to be/do will likely be the professional who ends up knowing and often controlling all the client's investable assets.

The Big Purchase Factor

As a financial advisor, you can help clients enjoy their money more by helping them avoid the big mistakes on major purchases. Personal finance resources have no shortage of tips for managing your spending: pack your lunch instead of eating out; brew your own coffee instead of stopping at Starbucks. Yet clients often dig a tremendous spending hole because of their big purchases, and then worry irrationally about the small stuff, trying to make up the difference. If you really want to change your clients' financial reality for the better, focus on the big stuff—where they live, and what they drive, the upkeep of their home and the status symbol of their car.

Consider recent information from the Department of Labor about *Where Does The Money Go* for the average household. If we add up all of the Housing categories and sub-categories, and add transportation on top of it, we come to a whopping 63% of the household's total annual expenditures. Entertainment? Only 5.5%. Clothing and apparel? 3.5%. Food is almost 13%, but we can only trim so much, since we do still have to eat a little every day.

So why do we focus so much of our spending advice on things that constitute barely 20% of our spending (entertainment, clothing, and food) and so little on the 60% and more that goes towards transportation and shelter? The truth is, we buy the most expensive house and car we can afford, and then drive ourselves crazy clipping coupons to make up the difference. Perhaps the better conversation is about owning more affordable houses, and driving less expensive—or, dare I say it—*used*-cars.

I think this is especially important in light of the growing body of research that shows how so much of the happiness we derive from our financial well-being is about spending money on experiences, not stuff. So why do we still tell people to give up the experiences they enjoy—eating out, going to the movies, and their morning Starbucks routine—and never acknowledge that if you buy a $20,000 used car instead of a $35,000 new car, the $15,000 in your pocket pays for all of these enjoyable experiences, and much more? Along the same line, choosing an apartment that's $500/month less expensive or a smaller house that represents $500/month less in mortgage costs saves so much money on "the big stuff" that many wouldn't have to sweat the small stuff at all anymore. Ironically and sadly, the more affluent the individual, the more those significant housing and automobile costs consume huge portions of their annual income.

These are difficult conversations to have with our clients. Many people view their nice homes and their nicer cars (one, two, or even more of them) as entitlements that they *should* get the moment a lender will approve them for financing. The research shows, however, that maxing out your capacity to borrow might not lead to a default, but it certainly does crowd out your ability to spend money on the experiences that ultimately bring us more happiness.

When it comes to advising clients, have the conversation about a change in residence or a "new" automobile if you think it would improve their quality of life. Take a few moments to make them think about the trade-off. A modestly smaller automobile can save so much money, they may not have to sweat the small stuff anymore. It is amazing to me how many Americans do not realize that most new cars can go well over 100,000 miles.

As long as there's a secure roof over your head, and you have an automobile that's capable of getting you to work and getting the kids where they need to go —even if that car isn't as fancy as you hoped, or the house isn't as big as it might have been—life will go on. And you'll probably enjoy it more when you can splurge on pleasurable things and quit worrying about your debt load.

Longevity: Your Client's Greatest Risk

Be careful what you wish for. A husband and wife in their early 60s were celebrating their 40th wedding anniversary in a quiet, romantic little restaurant. Suddenly, a tiny yet beautiful fairy appeared on their table. "For being such an exemplary married couple and for being loving to each other for all this time," she said, "I will grant you each a wish." The wife answered, "Oh, I want to travel around the world with my darling husband." The fairy waved her magic wand and poof! Two tickets for the Queen Mary II appeared in her hands. The husband thought for a moment: "Well, this is all very romantic, but an opportunity like this will never come again. I'm sorry my love, but my wish is to have a wife 30 years younger than me." The wife and the fairy were deeply disappointed, but a wish is a wish. So the fairy waved her magic wand and poof! The husband became 92 years old. The moral of this story: Men who are ungrateful should remember fairies are female.

The joke is funny, but notice we accept the age 92 without much thought. Age 92 is common today. Tomorrow's life expectancy will be age 100. For some strange reason, even though most clients know people who are 92, they don't think about, or plan on living into their 90s.

Take a couple in their early 60s; they could have three decades to make their money last: that is 30 years—almost half of their lifetime again. Longevity statistics suggest that they are going to live longer than they think. Planning for age 100 is already happening. The greatest risk to people's investments is not the markets, their investment choices or even their behavior (e.g., their propensity for buying high and selling low.) Their greatest risk, which their advisor cannot control, is longevity.

The value you offer is your ability to advise clients on how much they can spend now without regretting it later. This leads us into the discussion about how much clients should take from their accounts.

The Withdrawal Game

To avoid future regret, one needs to be mindful of today. I believe the flexible approach would be a withdrawal rate that varies from two to six percent (2-6%). Professionals often say the withdrawal rate doesn't have to be set in stone. When the portfolio is riding the highs of a bull market, the rate may be able to be boosted to five or even six percent. Taking out big chunks after a crash like that of 2008, however, can do long-term damage; you're withdrawing money when the markets are close to a low point. Dialing the rate back to 2 or 3 percent when stocks are down gives the portfolio a chance to potentially recover.

Planning must consider the sequence of returns, and not just average returns.

It astonishes me how badly we fail in math. Einstein says compounding interest was one of the most fascinating things he ever studied. We have to look at the data correctly.

I need to note that the following scenarios are hypothetical in nature and are provided for informational purposes only. They are not intended to represent any specific return, yield or investment, nor are they indicative of future results.

Investment A has a three-year performance as follows: Year 1, it goes up 100%, thus doubles; Year 2, it goes down by 50%; and year 3 it goes back up 25%. Thus investment A for this three-year period has an average return of +25%. (Math: 100%+(-50%)+25%=75% divided by 3 years = 25%).

YEAR	A – RETURN
1	+100%
2	-50%
3	+25%
Average	+25%

Now compare Investment A with Investment B's three-year performance as follows: Year 1, Investment B goes up +8% and does the same for year 2 and year 3. So investment B for this three-year period has an average of 8%. (Math: +8%+8%+8%=24% divided by 3 years = 8%).

YEAR	A – RETURN	B – RETURN
1	+100%	+8%
2	-50%	+8%
3	+25%	+8%
Average	+25%	+8%

Now ask yourself the important questions. If this was all you had to go on to make a decision regarding which investment you wanted, which investment would you choose? Which investment would most clients choose? Most people would see this and choose investment A, because the average return is more than triple that of Investment B and therefore it must be a better investment and would be expected to make the client more money.

Albert Einstein called compounding interest the eighth wonder of the world. "The most powerful force in the universe is compounded interest." Please slow down and take this in. Albert Einstein, the brilliant physicist who helped develop the nuclear bomb thought that compound interest was so powerful that he was amazed and in awe of the complexity of how it worked. Let me continue my example to help you see why that might be true.

To determine which of the above investments is really better, you must apply a dollar amount, or purchase price, to the investment. In the end, the client is more concerned about how much real money they will have at the end of the time period under consideration. So, let's make a $100 purchase each in Investment A and B.

Investment A with $100 invested in the first year goes up 100%, thus doubles and grows to $200. Then in the second year it does down by -50% and loses half of the $200 to end the year back where you started at $100. Then in the third year, the $100 goes back up +25% to end the year at $125. Thus the total profit of the investment for the three years is $25. (Math $125 - $100=$25)

Investment B with $100 invested in the first year goes up 8% to $108; then in the second year, it goes up another 8% to $116.64 and then goes up another 8% to $125.97 in year 3. Thus the total profit of the investment for the three years is just under $26. (Math $125.97-$100=$25.97)

YEAR	A – RETURN	$100	B – RETURN	$100
1	+100%	$200	+8%	$108
2	-50%	$100	+8%	$116.64
3	+25%	$125	+8%	$125.97
Average	+25%	+8.33%	+8%	+8.65%

The mistake we make in thinking that average return is actual return is perceptual. If we apply the average return for Year 3 to each investment respectively, the difference is clear. If Investment A had maintained a 25% return for each of the three years consecutively, the resulting total would have been $195.31. Variable returns can significantly impact long-term results.

The importance of this sequence of returns makes a huge difference, because the average does not mean the actual. The most important part of past performance is the sequence of how the returns were derived. What is amazing to me is how an investment with a lower average return in real dollars can outperform an investment with a higher average return, all based on the sequence of returns.

Show this to clients sometime. At first glance, Investment A looks really good compared to Investment B. How can an annual average return of 8% possibly yield the same amount of income over three years as an average return of 25%? Yet the net is almost the same (actually a little more). That blew my mind! I still play with the numbers to make sure it's right. Another problem with Investment A is that many investors wouldn't have stuck with it anyway. Even after fabulous returns the first year, many would have jumped ship after the second year nosedive. You want to give clients the smoothest ride possible so they don't jump off the cliff. Most are not as tolerant of wide swings in the market as they think they are.

It's interesting that the sequence of returns is, in the end, what grows your clients' money more than some average return.

The truth is lost in the average. What average annual returns don't tell us matters a great deal. If you and your client only had two portfolios to chose from and they had the following average annual returns, which one would you and your client choose?

	1 YEAR	3 YEAR	5 YEAR
Portfolio A	47%	16%	8%
Portfolio B	8%	8%	8%

With this information, Portfolio A appears to have superior historical performance, but you know from the truth of the historical 5-year average averages that there might be another way to look at this. What if we could see the annual sequence of returns.

Actual returns reveal that portfolio A was more a onetime wonder than an investment with superior historical performance. Additionally, we learn that to add money to Portfolio A would be to buy high and lock in someone else's gain rather than making a wise long-term investment.

More importantly, it is not wild returns and risks that can compound your money; it is more the consistency of those returns. The more consistent and steady the sequence of returns, the more powerful the compounding. Thus, the main point of all this is to stop chasing performance.

Stop Chasing Performance

Performance chasing is not a good investment strategy. When an investor suffers from performance chasing, he or she perceives trends where none exist and then takes action on these erroneous impressions. People tend to look for patterns and attribute trends to methods other than simple chance.

When selecting a money manager, a one-year return (or attractive returns for the past few years) could cause clients to drop their current money manager in favor of the "hot" manager. This can lead to dangerous assumptions and predictions, when investors should be focusing instead on the advice and ongoing planning of their financial advisor. Let your clients focus on what they need and want in the short term and for life by explaining to them you are responsible for the investment allocations, diversification and the rebalancing for both, with an overlay of distribution planning for when funds are needed.

Investor returns for almost any given investment support the theories about investors' poor timing. An investment's net cash flow history tells the story: Investors piled in during its run-up, with most inflows occurring near the investment's peak. Investors then fled as the returns plummeted, with most outflows occurring near the investment's bottom. In fact, investors were still leaving as it rebounded and consequently were not around to recoup some of their losses.

Chasing yesterday's performance seems to be a business model. It might work for selling products, but it doesn't work for helping clients. Take 1990, when the top-selling sector of the market was Large Cap Stocks, based on how much money flowed into this area of the market. Trouble came with the Gulf War, along with a small recession. In 1990, the top-performing investment was cash/money markets. Since money markets offered the best return in 1990, sales took off in 1991. The media preached safety, the news was all about how bad things were, so not surprisingly, the top selling investments in 1991 were money markets. It did well the year before so it must be the right place to be now, right?

Wrong. In 1991, the best performing area of the market was *not* money markets; it was Small Cap. Look at the pattern in the following chart. One year's top-performer becomes the next year's top-seller, but in only one year out of eight was the top seller also the top performer. This is chasing yesterday's performance with no benefit for today or tomorrow.

Chasing Yesterday's Performance

YEAR	Top Selling	Top Performing
1990	Large Cap Stocks	Money Market Funds
1991	Money Markets	Small Cap Stocks
1992	Small Cap Stocks	International Stocks
1993	International Stocks	High Yield Bonds
1994	High Yield Bonds	Money Markets
1995	Money Markets	Small Cap Stocks
1996	Small Cap Stocks	Large Cap Stocks
1997	Large Cap Stocks	Large Cap Stocks

Source: Performance data from Simfund.

The real problem came later. If you invested in the 1996 top performer in 1996 (Large Caps), you were right in 1997. In fact, Large Cap was the right place to be for two more years. From 1997 through 1999 Large Cap Stocks were the top selling and top performing investment. All of a sudden this seems easy. Just own some large cap stocks and nothing else and you're set, lulled into a sense of security. Who needs an advisor? Online trading and do-it-yourself investing had come about because it was easy, performance numbers were easy to find, and everyone who used past performance as a guide was right. At least for awhile.

Then came 2000. Although for three years from 1997 through 1999, Large Cap was the best performing sector, that area of the market got crushed from 2000 to 2002 and took out most people who, in the end, never got positive performance.

I do not seek to be right in the investment choices defined as the best performing. I seek to not be wrong. Your clients need you to be different than the herd.

Average investors are underperforming their own investments because they are getting in and out of them at the wrong time. "Oh, I'm worried. Let's get a little more conservative." So you pay to get out and you pay to get back in, resulting in a permanent loss to the portfolio. I used to have a problem charging clients a flat fee until I realized that I believe I could help them achieve better performance by helping them stay invested when they needed to be.

The point here is simple: performance is poison. A poor track record for performance can be proven by math, but math can be confusing to some people. Our job is to understand the math and explain it clearly. The problem is that it is so much easier to sell past performance. The other problem is there are a lot of sales being done off past performance.

Furthermore, even if you can identify the best performers, it might be just before they become the worst. You cannot pick the best all the time, so don't try to add value based on trying to pick the best.

Make the ride for your client as smooth as possible to help them accomplish their goals. Here's what I ask them, "If you can accomplish your goals, does it really matter how you are invested?" Many just want to know what they can spend, what they can purchase, and want to be able to live without future regrets.

Don't allow yourself to get into past performance conversations, and certainly don't try to prove your past performance. Let me show you an example of what I'm talking about. I had a great CPA friend, Mike, refer a client to me. When the client came to our first meeting, we went through my process for initial meetings (defined later in the book). The next day this CPA sent me a one-sentence email which read:

Do you have any comparison of your model portfolio's performance for the past number of years?

When you know your value, this is how you can respond:

> *"Respectfully, I don't accept the premise of your question that I can add value to my clients by showing past performance. I understand why you asked, but let me offer you a few things to think about that will explain how we work and, more importantly, how we add value for our clients.*

A client must give us trust for us to do our job. The trust in the end must be freely given, and then it is our job to earn and keep that trust to keep the client. Trust, being an emotion, is not justified by some percentage number or performance. If that trust is not offered in the beginning, then we don't work with the client. Additionally, we will not seek to prove or convince someone to trust us; they either do or they don't. As we work with clients, our job is to earn and keep that trust. We do it by listening to them, customizing a plan to meet their needs and dreams, and then ensuring they stick with that plan. Thanks for reminding me who we are and aren't.

Mike's response to my email was, "thank you for reminding me why I send clients to you!"

Know your value and know it is not about proving something that happened in the past.

Asset Allocation and Diversification

"The No. 1 Job is not to make a lot of money. It's to control risk!"
                              – May 2011 Cover of *Institutional Investor Magazine*

There are plenty of financial representatives trying to sell their way to personal success—the ones who have the hot idea, and tell you they know what no one else does. But, if you want to stand out from the crowd, I believe all you have to do is offer investment options that are always and forever asset allocated and diversified—and, then, automatically rebalanced to stay that way. This is truly amazing to me.

The wonderful news about giving a client the smoothest ride possible is that this approach that has been proven reliable from studies and research done on 100 years of historical actual returns. The only problem is that it is extremely boring. There is nothing sexy about having your eggs in different baskets. But most clients just want to live their lives without worrying about how hot and exciting their portfolio looks.

A study of large pension plans showed that asset allocation accounted for 91.5% of the variation in a plan's quarterly return. By comparison, investment selection and marketing timing – factors that many investors believe to be important – accounted for just 4.6% and 2.2% respectively (Source: Brinson, Singer and Beebower, *Financial Analyst Journal*, May/June 1991). In spite of research proving that the old tried-and-true stewardship principles still work in today's financial world, in actual practice, they are the exception rather than the norm.

Typically, there is always something that outperforms a diversified portfolio. There is always something in the portfolio doing very poorly. That is the nature of diversification, and just a financial fact of life. And, naturally, your client will want to mess up the parts by moving what is doing poorly to what is doing well. As the advisor, it is your job to see that this does not happen.

So, how do you position yourself to offer your best to the client? You must choose to position the asset allocation and diversification strategy to clients as all or nothing. In other words, Mr. Client, you are not allowed to change the internal pieces of the pie. You must always and forever accept the whole, and let go of analyzing the parts. Why? That's the price that you must pay.

Report card logic does not work well with your investment portfolio. Taking your investments and grading them like you would your child's report card is a mistake. Let's use Junior's report card as an example.

Junior's Report Card

English	A
History	A
Science	A
Math	B
Finance	D

Now as a parent, if Junior brought this report card home, what are you going to talk about? The child psychologist would tell you to affirm the good behavior and congratulate him on the A's. However, we all know that at some point, we are going to have to discuss the D. In doing so with all the logic, love and wisdom, we are going to encourage the child to turn the D into an A. You need to improve, do better, etc. Now here is the mistake:

Too often, we apply the same report card logic to our investments. We want to take our D investments and make them A investments, but I believe this is exactly the wrong thing to do. Remember the old saying, "Buy low – sell high?" Well, that would mean you take your A investments and sell them to buy D-rated investments.

No one does this well. It goes against every fiber of your being. This is why you cannot let your clients judge their individual pieces of a wonderfully created, diversified portfolio. Why? Because Junior's grade point average is 3.2. (Math A=4 points, B=3 points and D=1 point thus 4+4+4+3+1=16 divided by 5 = 3.2)

Ask any client with kids this question: "If your child, for all the years he brought home a report card, had a 3.2 GPA, would you have been pleased? Would you be pleased with average or, in some cases, above average returns in your portfolio?"

All the client needs to see is the GPA, the average of the total portfolio. Encourage them to comment on how the average is doing. But, I recommend you stay away from discussions about the individual pieces of the portfolio. Human nature will lead them to move their D investments into A investments. Warning: If you let them repeatedly move into A investments, which have already performed well, you are actually allowing them to sell low and buy high. When you allow them to under-diversify their portfolio, and the A investment becomes a D investment, you lose, and so does your client.

Predetermined Investment Strategy

Leadership and productivity expert Bob Dunwoody has a wonderful question he asks advisors. "If you take your entire book of business, and assume you're sitting in cash—20, 40, 80, 100 million dollars in cash—where should it be invested?"

This was a wonderfully freeing question for me. Where should it be invested? Not where is it now or where has it been, but where should it be? The reason I can tell you, as I did above, that the vast majority of advisors do not apply an asset allocation and diversification strategy to their entire book of—and at a deeper level to every individual client household—is because the average financial representative has over 1,000 individual holdings. That's 1000 individual investments of which they may only follow or even know about 20 of them daily. Bob Dunwoody was trying to point out that each client is assuming you are watching their portfolio, but there is no way you can watch 1000 plus positions!

If your book was in cash and you decided where it should be invested, your solution becomes your goal for all past clients and future clients. Your goal is to create a predetermined investment strategy.

If I pooled every person I've ever worked with and reiterated their goals as simply as I can, they all would like to maximize returns and minimize risks. Many make the mistake of forgetting about risk until it shows up in a painful form that causes them to change their behavior. My recommendation is to come up with a predetermined investment strategy designed to diversify away as many risks as possible.

I recommend considering an investment strategy which avoids individual stocks, because in doing so, you can reduce individual business risks through diversification. Situations such as Pan Am Airways or Enron would be examples of business risk in their respective sectors. The BP Amoco Gulf Coast oil disaster is an example of business risk. Lehman Brothers is an example of business risk. The idea is to focus on a diversified pool of investments as you seek to avoid individual business risk.

Those are the academic reasons. Let's talk about the emotional reasons. Early in my career, I built a stock position in a well-known ketchup company.

That was back when I didn't really know what I was doing; looking back, no one else did either. Regarding this ketchup company, our firm's analyst went from a buy to a sell, based solely on the fact the stock had gotten ahead of itself and it was time to take the profit. On the basis of that short-term recommendation, which ended up being wrong, I called my client Betty, known by all as BaBa from the name bestowed upon her by the grandkids. When I told BaBa we needed to sell our position, she was very concerned and said she had to think about it. The next day she called me in tears. "Tyson, if we sell this ketchup company stock, I don't know what other brand I'm supposed to buy in the grocery store." By giving clients individual stocks, you give clients an emotional attachment of ownership, which works against them. When I sold a client out of an inherited position in Kellogg they had owned for years, they were happy because they could start enjoying other brands of cereal. Please know that stock positions may be influencing your clients' consumption habits, and they won't be objective when it comes to selling that stock. As I have said before, the business we are in is counterintuitive.

Again, I recommend that you set all your clients up with a predetermined investment strategy with the following attributes:

- The asset allocation should include at least 60% in equities for all assets not needed within the short-term (36 month) time frame.
- There should be exposure both to stocks and bonds, US, international, commodities, real estate, and multiple money managers.
- Set it up to automatically rebalance.
- Make sure quarterly summaries are available for clients.

I have two investment strategies based on the Nobel Prize-nominated studies for asset allocation and for behavioral finance by author Daniel Kahneman.

1. Set aside two years of living expenses (needed after fixed income amounts and considering big ticket purchases in the next two years).

2. Put the rest in asset allocation and seek to minimize taxes as much as possible into approximately a 60/40 stocks to bonds allocation.

In my opinion, the specific investments making up your allocation do not matter. It was startling to me when I realized the value was keeping the allocation the focus, not what was inside the allocation.

Long-term averages of a diversified portfolio will be long-term averages. Historically, so-called experts have not outperformed the long-term averages, in part because they are part of the average. So rather than focus on what does not matter—like the individual managers or specific allocation percentages—focus instead on what does matter: automatic rebalancing, multiple managers, and a commitment to invest for at least three years. This helps ensure both consistency and reduced volatility.

Regardless of their age, clients have two kinds of money: 1) the kind they need or want in the short term to spend and 2) the kind they need or want for their future (long term). Set aside what they need for #1 and invest the rest according to your predetermined strategy.

Beyond all the academic, fact-based, math-proven reasons to have a predetermined investment strategy for all clients, here's one more big one: You'll save lots of time. You won't have to do continuous research. You won't have to stay abreast of hot trends. Do what's best and save time too—a real win-win.

"Tyson," you may say. "What am I going to spend all my time doing if I don't talk about the markets or researching or trying to predict what the markets are going to be doing, or wiring 40-page asset allocation proposals to try to win new clients?"

Ahhh...now, *that* is the million-dollar question, because you will have so much more free time—time to spend on your "It list" you committed to on page 46.

What's Your "Value Add?"

You will add so much more value to your client relationships if you'll remember these things:

You Are Not A Savior: Do you see yourself as a hypothetical "savior" for your clients? This is a trap I myself fell into early on in my days as an advisor. A savior sets up a false expectation of what is possible instead of being brutally honest with what is possible and what is not. Trying to find a way to provide a client with a 6% or higher annual withdrawal rate to cover their annual income needs would be an example of trying to be a savior. To allow a client to think they can enjoy a lifestyle and "It List" which doesn't address the fact they may not be able to do both is trying to be a savior. I believe there is a savior, but we financial advisors are just not it.

Planning For Poverty: Don't take clients who are going to run out of money. Sue had $100,000 she had scraped together for her life savings. She was aggressively invested in stocks when I met her. I forced her to diversify, but she was already 70 years old and selling upholstered furniture. She suffered from arthritis and had a son who had gone blind. She had sold her house to a developer in exchange for being allowed to live rent-free. She was a beautiful woman who sang at church, but she consistently wanted to buy last week's winning lotto numbers (past performance). All along the way, I was being blamed because the account didn't do well enough. Of course, the reality was she hadn't saved enough her whole life, but now she had someone to blame. In cases like this, try to guide them through and let them choose their own course of action rather than give them someone to blame. You don't want to bear the guilt and shame of being blamed because they ran out of money. For these wonderful people, offer a plan of paying off all debts and putting their money in the bank until it is gone. If they are going to run out, they do not have the time to reap the rewards of long-term investing, so they shouldn't be investors and they should not be allowed to become your client. Set them free or join their prison of poverty. I don't take them on. I try to help them realize they need to accept reality, and investing is not what they should be doing.

Do Not Assume. Know: Do not make assumptions about a person's wealth.

In 2001, very early in my career, our office had an open house event. This very nice client, named Lois, showed up, but no one knew who she was. I was a young broker, willing to meet with anyone, and I set up an appointment with her. As it turned out, she had only a worthless penny stock in her account, which had been orphaned into the branch account, and was not assigned to an advisor.

I will never forget that first meeting with Lois, who had just retired at 80 years of age from being a librarian. She began by handing a piece of paper across my desk—a stock certificate—and asked the question, "Is this still worth anything?" What I held in my hand was 5,500 shares of Enron stock. My response to her question was, "I'm afraid not…maybe $500 bucks." Just 12 months earlier, before Enron declared bankruptcy, it had been worth over $500,000. I never bothered to bring this up because the damage was done. Why relive it? I did, however, ask how she had gotten the shares? She told me that her deceased husband had spent half of his life working for a utility company that merged over the years, and ended up being owned by Enron. Then, I asked her if she had any more of these certificates. "Oh, yes," she said.

It turned out that my little widow librarian, who had worked to age 80, subsequently deposited over $2,000,000 of stock certificates into her accounts. Those were sold, and she was moved into a predetermined diversified investment strategy, which I told her would help prevent the business risk of an Enron from ever happening to her again.

It is very dangerous to assume you know something because when you think you know, you stop asking questions. Knowledge may be power in some belief systems, but not in yours. For you, freedom is operating under the assumption that you don't know enough (especially about your clients), because you stay open to the possibilities and you keep asking questions. The best way to maintain your client relationships is to never assume you know the person. Keep asking questions to get to know each other. Clients will not always think to tell you what is important for you to know unless you ask them the right questions. Brokers claim to know everything about the markets, economies and investments, but they are not open to the possibility their clients don't care about what they know about these things. The majority of your clients do not want to know what a financial advisor knows; it is why they hire the financial advisor. What the clients want to know is whether they are on track, whether they will be okay or whether they will have future regret. Keep asking questions, and keep learning about your client's needs and helping your clients let go of worrying about markets, economies, and investments. Teach them to focus on thinking about—and sharing with you—what their needs and goals are. This is what I mean when I say your most important role is behavior management.

Speak Truth: Brutal, honest truth. If I can sum up my way of being in one sentence I would say, "I tell the brutal, honest truth." This does not mean only when it feels good, or when it is appropriate, or when it serves to benefit me financially. It means I tell the truth, all the time, to everyone. The problem with the truth is first you have to tell the truth to yourself about yourself. You might think that is easy. Does not everyone know the truth about himself? No, they do not. How many times have you said about one of your friends or family members, "He is just lying to himself."?

Prepare your clients for this honest approach. Always give them the pros and cons of what you're recommending or doing. One brutal honest truth is that most clients worry about the small stuff and are losing the big picture. Many need to fix their future retirements by downsizing their two biggest financial outflows: their home and their automobile. This may not be something they want to hear, but you owe it to them to tell them the truth.

Facts Vs Feelings: One of the things in dealing with clients and dealing with sales is to understand the very important difference between fact and feeling. I learned this from being married. When my wife is upset, I can give her all the factual reasons of why she has no justification whatsoever to be upset with me, only to find out the more facts I throw at the feelings, the stronger the feelings get, regardless of the facts. It is not until you actually identify and empathize with—or at least acknowledge—the feelings with words like "I understand how you feel," or "That really stinks," or "I'm sorry you're upset" that you can expect the facts to be understood. Always remember: No one really cares about your facts until you care about their feelings.

It Is Not About Being Right: I hate to disillusion you, but life is not about having to be right. As financial advisors, we're not supposed to be in the convincing business, though our powers of persuasion can certainly help when it comes to behavior modification. Do not play the game of having to be right. Help clients realize you're trying to get them closer to their goals and that sometimes they can get to the end goal without you having to prove you're right all the time. Focus more on getting them on the path and having them achieve the outcome than engaging in the "You were right, I was wrong" battle. Get clients acting more appropriately and stop worrying about getting the credit that you were right. I have found the less I focus on being right, the less clients focus on reminding me when I am wrong.

Student Teacher: How you define your role as an advisor is going to greatly define the value your client finds in you. Too many brokers hide underneath the title of financial advisor, trying to sell investments or market performance. These brokers spend their days talking about things they hope to be true, but the facts are the facts. I am a student of our profession, of planning and of distribution strategies. I am consistently seeking new ways to do things and help more people as my model grows.

Dangers of Over Control: A friend of mine who is a jet pilot once told me that whenever a jet goes out of control and begins to spin, the only thing to do is totally take your hands off the controls, and the plane will right itself. This goes against our natural inclination. We want to control and manipulate in order to bring things back under control, but usually the same principle applies in investing and in relationships. It is scary to be out of control, but on the other hand, try to think of it as a burden you don't have to carry.

Seriously Loosen Up: Do not take yourself too seriously. You really don't know what you are doing. That's okay, because nobody else knows either. We are all in this together, but we might learn from some very successful people like Warren Buffett who said, "I never met a man who could forecast the market." I assume he means he never met a man who could time the market or time individual investments in the market. Multiple studies confirm that investment success is about "time *in* the market" not "timing the market." Relax and let your predetermined plan work the way it's supposed to.

Compensate Yourself

How should you pay yourself? Should you get fee-based or transaction-based compensation? The problem is knowing whom to trust.

I have a philosophy about trust. Trust is given freely and earned in order to be kept or maintained. One of the best ways I earn trust is by being a fee-based advisor. Explaining to clients, "It costs nothing to hire me and nothing to fire me. You pay me along the way based on the value of the assets you have invested in your accounts and compensation is then based in direct proportion to how your account succeeds or fails." Though fee-based services may not be suitable for all investors, you can choose which investors you bring into your practice.

I like to use the example of a realtor when describing the difference between a fee-based and a transactional or commission-based broker. Realtors are paid based on the sale transaction. They get paid a percentage of the sale price of the house, but once the sale is over, they are no longer responsible, even if something happened like the house burning down or dropping in value within a few months. Realtors, like brokers, are still people and may even feel bad for a client who is negatively affected, but once paid, the broker and realtor are no longer financially tied to their advice. They have no vested interest in the financial success the client will have in living out the plan.

A fee-based advisor is much more accountable, because it puts everybody on the same side of the table as far as accountability is concerned.

A transaction-based system makes it too easy to take advantage of a client's emotions. For example, a client may say, "Tyson, I'm scared. Have you seen the headlines?" That makes it really tempting for me to let the client pull their money out of the market and put into cash, even though this might remove diversification or unbalance the portfolio. I'll appease the client and I will get paid for the transaction, but I would have put the client at significant risk of having a permanent loss when the headlines improve.

We think our job is to help people make money, but the truth is our job is to be better stewards of the money they have already made. As stewards, we should be paid more when the client makes more based on our advice and less if they make less, rather than being paid for each transaction we think we can justify.

It's ironic that the issue of compensation—fees versus commission, low cost versus higher fees—is not an issue to argue about according to data analyzed by software firm PriceMetrix Inc. (Spring, 2011 issue of *PriceMetrix-Insights*—http://bit.ly/pyNpZ6).

"The most surprising thing to us was the wide range of prices charged for similar relationships on similar-sized fee-based accounts," said PriceMetrix CEO Doug Trott.

The average fees charged progressively declined from 1.17% on accounts between $1 million and $2 million in assets to 0.63% on accounts with more than $5 million in assets. For accounts of between $250,000 and $500,000, the lowest quartile of the advisors charged an average fee of 81 basis points, while the highest quartile charged 208 basis points.

The transactional revenue on assets earned in balanced accounts of between $250,000 and $500,000 showed very little difference between low-priced fee accounts and the higher priced accounts.

"We conclude that pricing is not being driven by competition, because prices are all over the map. It appears that many reps are relying on hearsay from colleagues and clients in setting their fees," Mr. Trott said. A better strategy, he suggested, is for advisors to get information from their firm's back office on the average fees charged on all accounts at the firm—and price accordingly.

The data also dispelled the myth that lower-priced advisors are stealing business from their higher-priced competitors. "Those advisors doing the most business tended to charge more," Mr. Trott said.

Stop feeling guilty about making a lifetime impact! In part, advisors may be "guilt pricing," or lowering fees for existing clients to make up for perceived poor performance. The telling conclusion from the data, however, is that the demand for advisory services is not price-elastic. The satisfaction and loyalty of clients is also far more dependent on the advisor's sensitivity to the client's objectives and their effectiveness in communicating with and instilling confidence in clients about the investment process. "This is a high-value service," Mr. Trott said. "The message from this data is that advisors should charge more."

What are you worth? What difference does your advice make over the client's lifetime? If you help your clients accomplish all of their financial goals over the course of their lifetime, ultimately you are free. However, if you can help a client communicate what their money is for, document those objectives into a plan, and craft an investment strategy to meet those objectives, your compensation should increase if the investments appreciate, increasing the odds of the clients being able to accomplish their goals. Your compensation should decrease if they do not.

Interestingly, whether you are paid based on transactions or on advisory fees, this already happens, but you just didn't realize it. I still feel the best "value add" is a fee percentage of the assets under management.

Once you know who you are, what you want and the value you bring to those around you, all you have left is to help others do the same. The next section is about them, the clients whom you get to impact. The greatest impact is to help them learn what you have learned, to help them look in the mirror and discover who they are, what they want and how they can add value to their own lives and the lives of family, friends and this world. You get to help them do more than they can do on their own.

Now let us explore how to do that. Your world impact is about to expand.

PART THEM:
The Clients

....

Time is the coin of your life. It is the only coin you have, and only you can determine how it will be spent. Be careful lest you let other people spend it for you.

— Carl Sandburg

This section explores how you, the advisor, get to help your client use their "coin" to spend, invest and give. We realize we need to focus on what we know we can control. We know that we can control—or at least influence—our clients' important objectives, which are found in their hearts. In some cases, your job is helping them figure out who they are and what they want. Come alongside your clients and imagine being in their shoes for a moment. Think about the sacrifices they made in order to have what they have. Then have long conversations about what they have and what they think they want to do with it. What is the future for? What is the money for? Early in my career I learned about the acronym FORM.[1]

Client Relationships Take FORM

F.O.R.M. is at the heart of everything we do with money.

F: Family O: Occupation R: Recreation M: Mission

1 Duncan MacPherson (http://www.paretosystems.com)

Our passion is to understand the FORM our clients' lives are taking. Every time I talk to a client, my goal is to connect with them on each of these four topics. I don't waste any time talking about markets, investments or numbers. I talk about what matters to them. I focus on what they value. FORM is fundamental to every process and interaction I'm going to share with you.

In this section, I'm going to talk about how you value them through FORM relationships and FORM service to discover what their core values are—to discover the real them—because the relationship is more important than any other aspect of business. Take care of building relationships—true honest relationships—and everything else happens as a natural and wonderful consequence. When people feel valued, you will naturally acquire them as clients, not because of any sales process, but because they want to continue the relationship in which they feel important.

FORM Relationship

Live each season as it passes; breathe the air, drink the drink, taste the fruit, and resign yourself to the influences of each.

– Henry David Thoreau

Again most of your job is really getting a clear answer to the question: "What is your money for?" To get the answer to that question, however, you have to ask deeper, different questions to learn all you can about the person behind the money. FORM (Family, Occupation, Recreation and Mission) gives you the perfect framework for doing that. The whole focus is to spend as much time as possible learning about your client's past, present and future thoughts around his family, work and fun. Once you know what the money is for, make sure the client understands "they can have *it* all" once they know what "it" is. Remember the world tells them "they can have *it* all," but the focus is on "all." This is like being in prison—a horrible way to live, and you are never happy. Once you have helped the client identify what "it" is *for them* (and *it* is almost always a list of things) and how much money will be needed for *it*, then the rest of the money can be for their life mission. In the end, helping clients achieve what they want is worthwhile. Once they have covered their life list of "it", it gets really exciting when you can help them realize how they may be able to impact the world through a personally funded life mission.

There is a mutual connection as we travel through life together with our clients, and the best client relationships are those in which we get to be excited for each other, those in which clients are far more than clients. They are certainly not numbers. They are like family. In this type of client relationship, we get to cry, laugh, and celebrate together. In short, we share life. What an honor. Not everyone is meant to be in meaningful relationships, and certainly not everyone is meant to be in relationship with *you*, but when you can build this kind of trusting, sharing relationship with clients, you build the ability to have the greatest impact in their lives. Never forget that as you increase your ability to impact the lives of others, you increase the ability for your own life to impact the world in wonderful and unexpected ways.

"All-In" Relationships[2]

Treat every prospect and client as though you expect him or her to be lifelong devoted clients, because many of them will be. This kind of relationship will only happen, however, if they sense that you're genuine and that you can be trusted. Make sure they know you will take the time to really listen to their most precious dreams and goals and do your best to make them happen. When you're in a relationship—whether with your spouse, kids, friends or clients—go all in. Remember I talked about the relationship percentage game that most people think is 50/50? They're wrong. It's got to be 100% plus. Most people believe in the concept of fair and thus look at life as half full or half empty. They live their relationships in terms of fairness and seek to make sure they match what the other person is putting into the relationship. They also make the mistake of measuring what they put

2 Bob Dunwoody (http://www.bob@bobdunwoody.com)

into the commitment based on what someone else is putting in. Here's the flaw in that: you can't control other people; you can only control your own actions. Thus the only thing you should focus on is what you can put into a relationship. When you've got the 50/50 mindset, not only is the best possible outcome 100% or less, but once you've done your part, you tend to start judging whether or not the other party in the relationship has done theirs. That's fair, right? Fair maybe, but neither satisfying nor productive when you're wasting emotional energy on keeping score. Ironically, if you only focus on maxing out what you can put in and expect nothing in return, you might find yourself enjoying your relationship again. You'll also find that the richness and satisfaction from this kind of relationship adds up to way more than 100%. All in at 100% sustains and grows relationships. What a difference!

A New Paradigm for Prospecting

When you adopt the "all-in" attitude, suddenly prospecting is no longer selling. It is understanding with crystal clarity who you really are and what value you really bring to your clients. Then just be yourself. People do not want to be sold anything. To be sold is to do something you didn't really want to do. That is not what people want. They just want something to believe in. The Poison Rock Band got that song right, "Something to Believe In." It is being full of the truth about the value you provide others through planning that solves behavior management problems. It is helping prospects understand that you have the solution everyone needs, and you can't help yourself but to tell them about it. Enthusiasm and authenticity are definitely contagious.

FORM Service

When work is what you love to do, it's not work—it's serving.

— Alan Mulally, CEO of Ford

If we all get to invest in the same market and use the same investment strategy, then it has to be how you service your clients that will make you different. Here is the secret to FORM service—have fun. Don't work…play. You should not work your relationships, and you certainly do not "service" them. You enjoy them.

Consistent client experience is one of the primary goals of my practice. Making sure all your clients go through the same process is important. All the processes I'm talking about ultimately do the same thing—lead your clients to behave in ways that have the best potential for getting what they need in the long term.

My client service process seeks to have the client become unconscious regarding their investments, the markets and finances. The only thing I want the client to focus on is FORM: their Family, Occupation, Recreation and Mission. I try to spend little or no client time on financial updates. I focus, instead, on their life updates. I have found making them unnecessarily focus on their finances may cause them more harm than good. Thus, I believe what I call "unconscious investing" is the best way to keep them accumulating wealth and staying focused on the things that really matter to them. They are probably hiring a financial advisor to take care of their wealth because they do not want the burden of doing it themselves—or cannot do it themselves. They do not realize it, or use this terminology, but the end goal for all clients I have met is to help them be unconscious.

Giving an example is the best way for me to describe why being too focused on finances (too "conscious") harms the client. Let's assume you need to buy a refrigerator. Now before you decided you needed a new refrigerator, there were refrigerator ads everywhere—TV commercials, billboards and other advertising—but you were unconscious towards them because you didn't need them. As soon as you need to buy a refrigerator, however, you start noticing refrigerator ads everywhere, and they are conflicting and confusing. The same thing happens when clients are too conscious of their finances. They start watching the gyrations of the market every day. Soon they begin to lose the 30-year perspective you've worked together to set up for them and they want you to take actions that screw up their strategy.

Ongoing client service should not include surprising them with some market update or portfolio review. Rather it should be an ongoing, purposeful conversation on how their plan allows them to avoid worry and tying their emotions to the markets.

The top two reasons why clients leave their advisor is lack of communication and lack of trust; so the next time you lose a client, ask yourself these questions:

- Did they hear from you?
- Do they trust you?
- Are you worthy of their trust?

Who you are and the value you bring should create trust with the client. The best clients say, "I trust you with my life savings and I believe that you will help me maintain my lifestyle so I will not run out of money." Make sure you're the kind of advisor who has earned this confidence. Once it's earned, remind them of what you are doing for them.

In a review call with a great client of mine named Bill, he asked me the question, "So what is the good news?" It was the summer of 2011. There was no good news. The US debt ceiling was in gridlock in Washington; unemployment was over 9%; every day the news made it sound like our world was going to end. So his question was both profound and simple: "What is the good news?"

My response was quick and to the point: "The good news is the plan you and Ann created and are following allows us to take our focus off of short term headlines. In my opinion Bill, you don't have to worry about the current news." There was a long period of silence on the other end, and then this man—who had worked hard for 35 years to reach this point in his life—responded all choked up saying, "That really is some good news." Then I heard, "Hey Ann, we have nothing to worry about." I could feel his smile as he said those words.

Most financial reps would have spent a lot of time discussing the different events, headlines and current affairs, offering their opinions on predicting outcomes which no one can really know. In the end, Bill was asking for the only answer I was able to give him. I am paying attention so he does not have to pay attention. We have a plan that helps us react to the FORM data we know, rather than reacting to the fear of the unknown.

Process-Driven Client Service

Here is what I say about the 5 steps to a process-driven client service, all geared toward creating a system that works without their being conscious of it:

1. **F.O.R.M Interview:** This is an informal interview. By discussing where you are and where you want to be, we seek to identify how we may help and whether we are a good fit for you.

2. **Research and Evaluation:** Upon mutual agreement that we are the right fit for you, we review your current positions, allocations and saving patterns to provide recommendations for retirement strategies.

3. **Solutions and Fit:** We discuss the status of the progress you have made thus far and what changes may be needed to get you where you want to go. Your plan is created.

4. **Implementation:** Working together based on the results of step 3, we lay out the action plan needed to align your money to help achieve your goals. Your plan is put into action.

5. **F.O.R.M. Monitoring:** As your primary financial advisor, we regularly repeat steps 1-4 to advise you through life transitions. Your plan is monitored and adjustments are made as we and you deem necessary.

This process is for both prospects and existing clients. Everyone is going through the same process. We will discuss the specifics as they relate to prospects later.

Go Get Rehired!

In 2002, I sat every client down and told them I wanted to reapply for the job of being their financial advisor. I explained my desire to create a reoccurring, consistent client experience that also gave me the greatest opportunity to enhance how I could help them achieve their stated goals.

Here's the gist of what I said to each client in that meeting:

If you need to work with a broker who makes changes to your portfolio every time the headlines change, then you need to rethink working with me.

If you need to work with a broker who generates new hot ideas to sell you, then you need to rethink working with me.

If, however, you want someone who is 100% focused on building a trusted relationship that focuses on what your money can do for you, how your money can improve your life as you desire and help you avoid as much future regret as possible, then I am your advisor.

I will never call you about your accounts, the markets, and the investments specifically unless the situation dictates that I must. You hired me to worry about that, and I will take care of investments, markets and all things associated with those things. I have learned it does neither of us any good to involve you emotionally with these things, and from this point forward, I will not involve you. If you want to discuss your concerns, I am here, but please know that I am regularly in touch with other investment professionals, economists and experts to help make sure we are doing the right things with your money so I don't have to bother you with it. Agreed?

So Mr. and Mrs. Client, here is what I am going to do. I am going to seek to have a process-driven service system where I contact you quarterly, regardless of what's going on in the world or the markets. Each quarterly contact is designed to enhance how I am able to advise you. The first contact each year will be a face-to-face meeting. In this meeting I want to ask for the right to pretend like I don't know you. I want to ask you every question I would ask someone who is brand new to me. I want to ask you every question as if I never knew you. Why? Because I don't want to assume the answer would be the same as when I asked the first time. Why? Because relationships fail when one party starts assuming they know everything about the other party and stops asking probing questions into how that person might have changed. We all change and our circumstances change, and I want to make sure I understand your desire and priorities today, not just the ones you had when we first met. Based on how this meeting goes, more meetings face-to-face may be needed.

Once this step is completed I will reach out and call you three months later. This will be a phone call to see how you are doing personally, to hear about how the family is doing, how work is going, how your golf game is—to hear about what changed in life since we last talked. It is also to ask if there is any reason we need to meet. If there is not, then I will ask what you have planned for the next three months.

Three months later will be a call to review your plan. It will have been six months since our face-to-face meeting, and this call will be a little more of a review of how we are doing, what needs to change and if we need to meet. Then after this process is completed we go back to another "how are you doing call?" in three months.

The Client Annual Process

- **Quarter 1:** The client(s) and I do an in-depth full financial review face-to-face.
- **Quarter 2:** Three months later the client gets a "How are you doing?" call.
- **Quarter 3:** Three months later I make a financial review via the phone contact.
- **Quarter 4:** Three months later, the client gets another "How are you doing?" call.

The result is that twice a year we are going to kick the tires and make sure the client's goals, objectives and desires align with how we have the money invested. Then in between, twice a year, we are just going to call and see how the client is doing, because he or she matters to us.

Control Your Calendar

I've learned an interesting thing about the process above. I have determined for myself I want to have four proactive client actions a day. That could be four face-to-face appointments or four phone calls (or a combination) but I want no more than four. I want to only schedule these daily actions four days a week, so I have three other days to catch up, enjoy my own life and be out of the office. Then, I only want to plan this service for three weeks a month, giving me a whole week a month to be free to catch up, take a vacation or just think and slow down. It works out beautifully. The quarterly proactive reoccurring service system—one review a year with three quarterly follow up calls—can be broken down across my whole practice in quarters.

It took 10 years to realize this strategy works beautifully: why not have all my face-to-face review meetings in the same quarter? I had been doing my review meetings randomly across the whole calendar year, but this was counterintuitive to my goal of a consistent process. So I changed it and starting in the months of February through April, I have all my clients' face-to-face meetings. Why February? I started originally in January but found out two things. First, all year-end statements are not printed and in the hands of clients until the end of January, and second, many clients are catching up from the holidays through most of January. The other reason I chose these three months to start my face-to-face meetings was it was cold and boring in Wisconsin where I lived, so I might as well work hard and be in the office when there is nothing to do outside In addition, it was tax season. Yes, tax season, when all our clients are meeting with their CPAs and thinking about their finances, so I thought it would be good to be doing the same (and when possible, catch them before their CPA advises something that maybe inappropriate). I have found this proactive time to be the best time to get clients to come in for a face-to-face review, because they have to do their taxes anyway!

Okay forgive me for outlining what may seem obvious. I still get very excited about this and the positive impact it has had on my practice and my life. If your entire quarterly face-to-face financial review meetings start in February and end in April, you spend the rest of the year on the phone. For the next nine months, you only have to make four phone calls a day for four days a week for three weeks each month. So, you take 48 clients a month and make three monthly rotating groups.

Let me start with the end and come back. Four proactive client actions a day x four days a week x three weeks each month x three months in the quarter (quarterly rotation) = 144 clients. You only need 144 people to work four days a week, three weeks a month and spend a lot of time out of the office with just a phone to call clients, and those phone calls can be made from anywhere. Now why would you want to be out of the office? For me, it is because I meet virtually all of my new relationships (clients) when I am out of the office. The more I am out of the office, the more I meet new clients. The future of our industry hinges on our ability to build these relationships. Even more important, your future impact hinges on getting out of the office.

The process-driven service is more about allowing me to get out of the office to find new clients than it is to keep the ones I have.

Okay so how do you implement this? Most computer contact management systems can do this for you, but I just came up with a little code that I add to each household's computer contact.

2-5-8-11	3-6-9-12	4-7-10-1

There are three codes for the three groups of 48 into which you will need to divide your 144 clients, thus about 48 clients in each month to keep the work flow even. Each number represents a month on the calendar, and each number in the four-number sequence refers to the month in a different quarter. As an example, the 3-6-9-12 code means that this household will be set up for a "Face-to-face" meeting in March (3), a "How are you doing?" call in June (6), a "Review" call in September (9) and another "How are you doing?" call in December (12). Also, in each code, the first number is the month of the "Face-to-face" meeting. The number "3" in 3-6-9-12 means March is the "Face-to-face" meeting.

These numbers and codes were picked for a reason. Face-to-face reviews are happening during tax season February through April. In these meetings, we are asking questions to get to know what has changed in the FORM of our client's lives. It is based on any of these changes that we will make decisions around their investments to help insure there will be appropriate cash flow when needed.

After setting this up and getting running, I later found a much easier way to accomplish this. Duncan Macpherson of Pareto Platform created a contact management system that can automate this for you. For more information go to www.paretoplatform.com.[3]

Phone Call Scripts

The "How are you doing?" calls happen over the summer months of May to July with a typical call going something like this: "Mr. Client, Tyson calling, how are you doing? It's been three months since we sat down and reviewed everything in your situation. I have no concerns about your investments as long as nothing has changed with your goals and objectives. What are you going to do for the summer?"

All the review calls occur around the transition of people coming off of summer mode and back into work, school and fall mode—August through September. Those review calls ask, "How was your summer? Got any plans for the rest of the year?" Now keep in mind it has been six months since your face-to-face meeting, so this call will also ask about their cash balances at

---

3 Duncan MacPherson (http://www.paretosystems.com)

the bank and whether their current income is meeting their lifestyle expense needs. I always ask them if there is anything we can do better for them.

Then, the last "How are you?" call happens in November through January. In this one, you'll ask "What are you doing for the holidays?" or "How was your holiday?" In this call we will remind them of their upcoming annual face-to-face meeting.

Always listen. Do not multitask while you are on the phone with them. Here is a tip that will help build loyalty and show your clients that you care. During every quarterly contact, try to find out what the client is going to be doing. It might sound like this: "Are you going to do anything fun in the next three months?" Their answer will give you an opportunity to cement the relationship. Suppose they mention that they're going on a cruise. Find out where they are going; spend $50 and have a bottle of champagne and strawberries sent to their stateroom. Suppose they're moving to a new home or apartment. Send them a doormat with their name on it. If they are going on vacation, go buy them a book about the destination. The goal of this is to make the client say to themselves, "Wow, I can't believe you thought of this."

I no longer spend much money on actual marketing. I spend most of my money on clients to give them the "Wow" experience they won't get elsewhere. My whole team seeks to create this "Wow" experience. My assistants have been recruited as secret operatives who, with just a few normal questions, can get enough information to surprise the client and make them feel special. The industry and firms set gift policies you need to respect, of course, but the "Wow" experience is more about how you do things than how much you spend. "Wow" is a lot of fun.

This scheduling process is the best thing I've ever done for my peace of mind to ensure continuity of care with my clients. I learned it from the dentist who schedules six months to a year in advance. I may not know what I'm doing six months in advance, but I still make the appointment and show up. I found out we are all trainable, both me and my clients. They know what to expect and when. Once their investment plan is in place, you don't need to meet in person more often than once a year, and this whole process encourages them to behave better than if they were thinking about their finances more often. They are moved to this service platform, and all we seek to do is make sure nothing changes in their family, occupations, recreations and mission in life. In other words, we want to make sure the FORM of their life hasn't changed, and then we "Wow" them. Try it. You will be a convert too.

How to Get More of Them:

Be careful about playing the game of more, because it's this game that causes us to try and go find new relationships at the expense of the relationships we already have. Make sure that in getting more clients, you don't lose existing clients in the process. When you really are sold out (e.g., your schedule is booked as outlined above), you're all in and focused on enjoying the relationships you have, all you need to do is tell others about how much fun you're having. Don't we all want to have fun? We all want to enjoy relationships with those who want the kind of relationship we offer, so it's important to look for the right kind of people to be clients.

I have found that when a client is surprised by my "Wow" attempts, they tend to tell their friends. Many times I have an initial meeting with a referral who says, "My broker doesn't pay attention to my life like you do for Bill's."

Who's Your Ideal Client?

We know we need to find 144 clients to serve (see page 105). We know how much money we want and that to do so, we need between $66,000,000 to $100,000,000 in assets under management (AUM) based on hypothetical fees of 1.00% to 1.50% (see page 44). That plugs us into the bottom line that we need 144 Clients who average around $500,000 dollars in assets.

$100,000,000 @ 1.00%= 144 Clients with $695,000 average AUM

$ 80,000,000 @ 1.25%= 144 Clients with $555,555 average AUM

$ 66,666,600 @ 1.50%= 144 Clients with $462,500 average AUM

We all have rich neighbors. One out of every 13 households in the United States has a net worth of at least $1 million, not counting the value of the family's primary residence (source: Joint Center for Housing Studies of Harvard University, Spectrum Group). Finding 144 households with half a million dollars should be easily attainable.

The industry makes us think we have to find huge high net worth clients. I wouldn't want them anyway. Most high net worth clients are high-maintenance and—what's even more important for me—I can't help impact their lives. If you have $5,000,000 or more, you probably don't need me. I can't make sure you don't run out of money; you have enough. But the client who has one or two million can run out if they're not careful. Those clients are the ones whose lives I can impact, and in doing so, I can change the world through them forever.

Change your paradigm and realize you do not need people with tons of money. You just need 144 people who have at least half a million dollars and need someone to help them make it last as long as possible.

Before you take on another client, ask yourself what kind of client you want to have in your family of clients. My client policy is comprised of ten expectations:

1. Client is an individual who wants to enjoy life and maintain his/her standard of living.
2. Client is not driven by money.
3. Client desires to build a relationship based on the trusted advice and exceptional service that I have to offer.
4. Client entrusts all their investable assets with me. This allows them to consolidate accounts and simplify records.
5. Client has investable assets of at least $500,000 or has a disciplined savings plan to get there.
6. Client is patient and understands the investment world is full of probabilities, possibilities, and that there is nothing certain about investing.

7. Client's job is to let us know when something has financially changed in their life or if they become concerned about an investment. Our job is to manage client behavior, expectations and risk in an effort to reach stated objectives.
8. Client respects our time and makes appointments in advance, allowing us to be prepared to meet with them.
9. Client knows our financial associates will gladly handle all service details and make all appointments.
10. Clients are advocates of our business and understand they are part of an exclusive family of clients.

To that last point, clients are told they are part of an exclusive family of clients. They are told we don't just work with anyone. We remind our clients and tell new clients we have a termination policy, usually because the client would no longer follow our counsel. It is a fact that we decide if we are going to bring on the client and keep the client. We're not trying to be artificially exclusive; it's a professional decision in everyone's best interest. It also keeps the client from getting an ego or forgetting we are the professionals.

Generally, I only meet with a potential client at the request of an existing client or a center of influence, but each of you must decide on your own level of exclusivity. We seek clients who are focused on value rather than cost.

How to Prospect

There have always been four ways to prospect

1. Make calls
2. Send mail
3. Public speaking (seminars, etc.)
4. Seek referrals

You should be doing all of them all the time, but keep this in mind: you need to find your voice first. The way I prospect is to share the past experiences

I have with everyone who will listen. If people don't want to listen, I go find those who will. By talking about who I am, what I believe, and how I define my values and processes to service my clients. It's not about asking them for their business—it's about telling them why you do what you do. When they understand you are motivated by *their* needs, goals, hopes and dreams, they begin to understand it's a partnership, not a sales job. In the end, if they don't already have this kind of relationship with their financial advisor, they want it.

Listen to me very carefully on this. I am talking about something that no one else is talking about.

When you help someone escape from the financial media and the compulsion to find the next hot idea—when you help someone actually put a plan to their money in order to help them avoid future regret—you had better stand up and tell the world.

When someone hears this and wants to have what you have to offer, stop and apply this process. Surprisingly, it's the same five steps to a process-driven client service we explained earlier.

1. **F.O.R.M Interview:** Informal interview discussing where you are and where you want to be, we seek to identify how we may help and whether we are a good fit for you.

2. **Research and Evaluation:** Upon mutual agreement that we are the right fit for you, we review your current positions, allocations and saving patterns to provide recommendations for retirement strategies.

3. **Solutions and Fit:** We discuss the status of the progress you have made thus far and what changes may be needed to get you where you want to go. Your plan is created.

4. **Implementation:** Working together based on the results of step 3, we lay out the action plan needed to align your money to help achieve your goals. Your plan is put into action.

5. **F.O.R.M. Monitoring:** As your primary financial advisor, we regularly repeat steps 1-4 to advise you through life transitions. Your plan is monitored and adjustments are made as we deem necessary.

Where do you start? Where do you get new clients—and how?

First, get the right mindset. You are setting out to create new relationships. Expect nothing more than an opportunity to tell your story, why you are passionate about your work and what you believe. Seek to get others to listen and ask questions, but don't expect them to become a client.

In fact, expect that they do no want what you are offering—they never thought that what you're offering might be something they needed. I like to get them to actually admit they have not thought about really having a plan that explains what their money is for. Or, that having a predetermined investment strategy which encompasses their entire financial picture was even possible. I like having a conversation to explain why I feel that the mistakes made in our industry can be addressed and solved by the plan I am could put in place for them. Expect nothing. There is still the question about whether or not they should even become a client. I might not even want them as a client. What you don't have, you can't lose. But you will get better at telling people what you do. And, along the way, you will start to attract the right kind of client to your practice.

Getting Past Hello

Whether you are attempting to meet someone new, or there is a couple who has been referred to you sitting on the other side of your desk, you need to know where to start. Relationships take time. So, let's review how you start when meeting someone for the first time. My first request is that they bring nothing to the meeting but themselves. Since the most important part of the meeting is getting to know the person, and not their financial statements, I explain that our interview is to get to know each other. If, after the interview, we both agree to move forward, we will ask for all of their financial information.

You might begin by telling them about yourself, your passion for this business, and the value you bring to the table. This should take only about five minutes, and might sound something like this:

My name is Tyson Ray, I am a financial advisor to a select number of families. I help them bridge the gap between what they want to do in the rest of their life and the resources they have to do it. I help them put a plan in place to help define what the future will look like so no one is surprised. My passion is to be able to sit down with clients in 20+ years and have them tell me I helped them improve the quality of their last 20 years. What will be the sum total of my career? It will be how clients tell me I helped them in the previous 20 years. That is my passion for my clients and the measure by which I measure my success; I feel it is also my "value add" and my accountability. In order to decide if we're a good fit for each other, I have a series of questions that will help me do two things: 1) get to know you and 2) explore what you are trying to do and how much money you have to do it.

Then I use the FORM process of exploring the possibilities:

- **F=Family:** Tell me about your family: Are you married? How long? How did you meet ? (Be sure to catch the anniversary date). How old are you? Do you have children? What are their names, birthdates, and status (i.e. married, grandchildren, etc.). Are there any special needs that must be considered (e.g., mental or physical disabilities of client or family members)?

- **O=Occupation:** Tell me about you current job or the job from which you retired. How long did you work or have you been retired? Why did you choose it? What other jobs have you had? Did you spend any time in the military? Where did you go to school? What do you want to do in the future for work, keeping in mind retirement is a job?

- **R=Recreation:** What do you for fun or hobbies? Where do you go to church? What charities do you support? What things do you do in the community? If there is some hobby you would take up if you had the time or the money, what would it be? Do you expect or want to travel extensively during your retirement?

- **M=Mission:** What kind of life mission do you have if any? How do you want to impact the world before you die? What does your estate plan look like? To whom do you want to leave your remaining money? Do you have any charities you want to include in your estate?

After spending maybe 30 minutes just asking open-ended questions, I move into the questions that will help bridge the gap between what they really want to do and how much money it will take to do it. I need to get a feel—and a best and worst case range—for when they want to retire and/or how much money it will take for them to retire.

In a Hollywood movie called *The Bucket List*, the two protagonists came up with a list of things they wanted to accomplish before they died. This term works handily in a planning conversations. I ask them to tell me what five things would be on their bucket list over the next ten years? How much would they cost, and in what order they would want to accomplish them? How much would they cost, and in what order they would want to accomplish them? Do they want to leave a specific dollar amount to their heirs?

Notice that this is the first money question after talking with these people for over an hour in what is usually a 90-minute session. I have spent no more than 10 minutes on what I do myself. The rest of the time is spent getting to know *who* sits across from me, not how much money they have. I start this series of questions like this, "Okay, now that I have an idea about who you are and what you are trying to accomplish, let's explore some specifics about what you have."

If they bring statements, I will not look at them in this meeting. I want them to tell me what they have. Going over statements can be a distraction or cause us to explore something in a depth that is not beneficial for this meeting. If they brought statements, I tell them, "Let me ask some questions first, and if you want to reference a statement that's fine. If we decide to work together, I will review the specifics in the statement later."

The Money Questions
- Where do you bank? What is the bank's name and how much cash do you keep on hand?

- What is your emergency fund balance (defined as cash, money markets and short-term CDs)?

- Do you have a personal banker who normally works with you, and what is that person's name? Please know cash—cash management is the greatest single asset a financial advisor can offer his clients.

- Do you own your home or rent? How much is the rent or the home worth? What loan balance is on the home and what is the rate? What bank has the loan and why? Do you have a plan or goal to pay off the house?

- Do you have a pension in retirement? If so, how much do you think it will pay you?

- Do you have a copy of your social security statements? Do you want to include Social Security benefits into your plan?

- Do you have a retirement plan at work? What company runs the plan? Is there an advisor over the plan? If so, do you know their name? How much is your balance? How much do you contribute?

- Do you have any old retirement plans and/or IRAs? What company runs the account? Is there an advisor over the account? If so, do you know their name? How much is your balance? How much do you contribute?

- Do you have any other real estate holdings? Rental properties? Business ownership?

- Do you have any investment accounts at the bank or financial firms? What company runs the plan? Is there an advisor over the plan? If so, do you know their name? How much is your balance? How much do you contribute and how often?

- Are we going to be giving your parents money or getting money from your parents? If you feel we are going to need to help financially support your parents, we need to plan for that. Also if you are expecting to receive some large inheritance, that is also something which would affect how I advise a client.

If they say along the way they don't know or have to dig into the statements, it helps show me how much they pay attention, how conscious they are about their investments, and how knowledgeable they seem to be about basic financial concepts. If they state specifics within each account balance or asset, I know they look at specifics. I will then know going forward, I need to be more specific. I will also see which spouse answers the questions. I want to know how they have delegated financial responsibilities between themselves. Does one spouse handle the big picture or just give approval and then the other spouse tracks specifics? Does one spouse handle everything while the other spouse has no idea what is going on? Does one handle the monthly bills and expense and the other handle the long-term money? These questions are designed to help reveal how a couple makes decisions and how I will work with them as clients. This is why I will not have this meeting unless both spouses are there.

Slow down and pay attention to how open they are. If you find they have an advisor, ask what they think of that person? Then every time you reference that account, don't refer to the account at Merrill Lynch, but refer to Mike (who is their advisor at Merrill Lynch). Having an advisor is a personal relationship, I make all references to other advisors a reflection on the person, not the firm.

Once we have gone through this series of questions, I end the meeting with this comment: "I am going to take 48 hours and process what you have just told me and ponder if I am the right person to help you bridge the gap between what you want to do and your resources to do it. At the same time, I want you to take the same time and ask yourself if you're ready to hire someone to be your sole financial advisor and to be responsible for a comprehensive plan over everything have. Are you ready to trust someone to not only help you make better investment decisions, but to understand how to save and/or spend as you need? Are you ready to have someone tell you the brutal honest truth and ask you, when necessary, to do what might be hard to do?"

My job is not to make clients my friends, but to help clients avoid mistakes. There are times I am able to help clients do the very thing they want to do like spend their money, but there are other times when I have to help them not do the very thing they want to do. I want to be my clients' trusted professional, much like their trusted doctor. The doctor is not there to be your friend, but your doctor. That doesn't mean we can't *become* friends and be friendly, but if you're my client, I am always your advisor first. You need to decide if you are ready for this.

I remember meeting Jon for our first interview meeting. Jon didn't know better; he had worked with three other brokers before meeting me. He started our meeting by opening up his three-ring binder, turning to its most recent statement and pointing at the $2,000,000 number. "This is what I have. Let's do the paperwork to move it over to you." I looked at him and said, "Thank you. We have a process of taking on new clients. Can we go through the process? He said yes, so I closed the three-ring binder, moved it to the side and starting learning all about Jon.

Jon had kept changing brokers, because everyone wanted to sell him something and didn't understand who Jon was. Jon moved his account only after we agreed I would be the first financial advisor he ever had and the last one he would ever need.

After the First Date

Yes, no (but not maybe) or I will think about it. After the first meeting, I will call the prospect in 48 hours and find out if we both agree to move forward. I explain that the answer is "Yes, we are going to go through our whole process" or "No, we are not." Maybe you want to think about a polite way of saying "No." Our Clients do not pay us to spend our time trying to convince or chase down non-clients who are undecided about the value we provide. If we agree to move forward, then the next step is a complete financial review. I will send them a large envelope with $4 of return postage on it with a letter explaining all the statements I want, recapping what they told me. Additionally, I ask for a copy of:

- Their will or trust and estate documents, including power-of-attorney and health care.
- A full copy of their most recent tax return
- A copy of their most recent life insurance, disability and long term care policies, if they have any.

I want to find out not only about the accounts, but also the type of relationship they have with current advisors, if any. If you need to say anything about service they have received from others, make sure you approach it from the standpoint of poor planning or lack of proactive service. Never attack the person.

In this call, I tell them if they do not get me this paperwork in the next few days, I will assume they are not serious about moving forward. I tell them I will remind them, but if in the next month nothing comes in to help us get started, I believe they are wasting my time and theirs.

Once they bring in the documentation a review is done on how much they have in assets and where it is. I quickly go over it to get an estimate of what their allocation looks like and what the costs, taxes and consequences would be to move what they have into my predetermined investment strategy. Everything that comes over is going into an investment strategy. I spend no time researching what they have their things in, because I am not in the proof or convincing business. If they are going to be my client, they are going to be in my recommended predetermined investment strategy in which I have all my clients. The only thing to research is how that can happen and what the client needs to know in order to allow that to happen. In the end, the clients are choosing to hire me completely.

There are fundamental mistakes I see advisors make over and over again in our industry:

- They let the clients choose the investment strategy.
- They try to sell value through investment selection or timing when there is no real value.

- They try to convince clients that their investment selection strategy is better than someone else's.
- They tell a client they can perform better than someone else when they can't possibly predict or control the factors that would allow that to be a true guarantee.
- They show clients past performance and allow the client to judge them based on how the past would have been.

I have to say, I love this one. I love when a prospect asks if I can send them some information on how my investment strategy has done. My response is "No." No, because Mr. Client, that is the most dangerous question you can ask someone to provide you, because I can go create the best performing investment strategy that ever was, and I can because hindsight is perfect. I will not show you what has happened in the past because the past doesn't matter. You are hiring me for your future. On a side note, if you ever come across a perfect portfolio of the best investments—five stars and there is no way to poke a hole in the strategy—ask the client how long they have owned the portfolio. Most likely it is not very long, because they were probably sold last year's best funds for a fee. They feel very good about how their account has performed. The only problem is they actually didn't get the performance. They're betting that past performance will continue. Ouch.

My answer is "No." You are asking me to go back and show you what I have done, but too many advisors go back into the past to build the perfect, best performing investment strategy of today for tomorrow. The problem comes, however, when the advisor needs to change that strategy. The advisor often has to get the client to rehire them by convincing them that the great thing they pushed last month is not going to work this month. This leaves the door wide open for the client to look for another advisor.

Make sure your client are hiring you, not your recommendations. Because you do not change. You stay the same, and if it's you they hired, you can change your investment strategy without having to get the client to rehire you every time.

Never forget that the client experience is based on what the money is *for*, and last year's returns do not explain what it is for. The small average rate of returns in the past has nothing to do with the stability of the future.

The Solution Meeting

Your next meeting is the "solution" meeting where you explain to the client what you heard in the first meeting. This is the meeting where you do a lot of the talking, asking the client to confirm that you understand what they are trying to do and how much money they have to do it. I explain how we manage money in predetermined investment strategies. I explain how their accounts could be moved into these strategies and what taxes, costs etc. will be incurred for making these changes. By using our investment strategies, they are hiring us to then manage and advise them on how to use their money. I then ask them how much information on the investments they would like to have to make a decision on hiring us. "How much paper would you like me to send for your kitchen trash can to explain why I believe these are the right investment strategies for you?" Most often the answer is none.

Stop trying to prove yourself. Remember there is no perfect, great is temporary, and good will get the job done. Specific investments shouldn't matter if they are part of a portfolio which is well-allocated, diversified, rebalanced automatically, and the client is not involved in the details of the strategy. Thus, the bottom line becomes whether they want to do it themselves or have you do it.

Sealing the Deal

Here is my closing question: "After everything we have discussed, are there any reasons you do not want to move forward?" If they have some, we discuss what they are and whether they should be a client at all. Once they agree to move forward, I explain we are going to take a few days to put the implementation paperwork work together. They will come back in or we will mail them the forms needed to implement the relationship. We try to have all forms signed in one sitting and explain why there may be a few stragglers. I explain we will have a meeting once all the funds have transferred over and have been put into our investment strategy. Thus, the second part of the implementation step is to review what has been transacted.

I tell them to keep anything they get in the mail. "We are about to send a tree through your mail box." Put everything you get for your old accounts plus everything we send to you about your new accounts in a bag and bring it with you to our next meeting. We will review it together and make sure we are all on the same page." I like to call this recap meeting the shred party.

At that meeting we recap the objectives, our role, why they told us they hired us, and why we have these investment strategies. We review all the mail they got and answer any questions they have if any. Then, once that is all done, we will then discuss whether any next steps are needed such as a review of the estate plan, life insurance, etc. If there are no other action items, we discuss our proactive client service schedule (annual meeting in person, quarterly calls, etc.). We tell the client we are going to monitor and worry about the investment and the items they have told us they want to accomplish in the next few years. If they have any concerns about these, however, they are feel free to call or we prefer you send us an email so we can then follow up. The email gives us time to research and prepare our response, thus saving both of us time. "However, Mr. and Mrs. Client, I do have something I want you to monitor and worry about. I want you to pay attention to the FORM your life is taking, to let us know if anything changes in your Family, Occupation, Recreation and Mission in your life. These are intangible things for which only you will know when they change. We expect you to over-communicate those changes to us. We are going to call quarterly just to ask if they have changed, but if the FORM your life is taking changes, it may require us to make changes to your finances, so we want to know right away."

There you have it: a plan that is clear, executable, and proactive—one that allows for the development of a solid advisor-client relationship in which they can rest comfortably that future needs have been considered and incorporated into the strategic plan.

THE END:

The Beginning

....

Prudence: Consideration of the future result of your present action.

In 2010 my oldest client to date passed away at 98. She was also my friend Chris, and her life became my truth for long-term investing. Chris became my client when she was 84. She was already in assisted living, and there was not much I could do for her. However, there was a lot Chris did for me. Her life was my lesson.

Chris had invested early and often. She amassed wealth and then taught me her best lesson at the end. Chris spent the last two years of her life sitting in an assisted-living residence. I visited and sat with her often, and she talked with me about her life in two very distinct paradigms. One of the paradigms centered on the theme of happiness and celebration. Chris recounted all of the things for which she was thankful and all of her wonderful and exciting experiences.

The other paradigm was that of regret. She recounted to me in grave detail all of the things that she wished she had done. To my amazement, Chris would have traded all of her money and stuff for better memories!

Ironically, many of the regrets Chris contemplated could have been purchased with her money if she had chosen to do so, but her advisors at the time never thought in terms of helping her avoid future regrets. The trade-off to have more money now was not worth it. The extra couple hundred thousand dollars in her account at the end of her life did not seem worth the things she put off or thought she couldn't do. She wished she had an advisor who might have encouraged her to spend more along the way so she wouldn't be saying to me at the end, "I cannot take it with me, my kids are fine, I wish…" This was such avoidable regret.

Chris and other people like her are, in the end, telling us where to begin. They tell us what our job really is and is not. As I learned from Chris and now share with you again, our job is not about making more money for our clients. Chris had money, but she would have traded it for more of a life.

What's It All About?

I want to help my clients avoid future regret, and I want you to be the kind of financial advisor who does the same. As financial advisors, we can come work side-by-side with our clients and advise them through their decisions. We help them realize the money that they've worked their whole lives to accumulate should be used to help them live their one life in the best and most meaningful way they can.

So that's why I wrote this book and why I preach this message every chance I get: I want you to be the best You possible so your clients can live the best lives possible. I hope I've equipped you with some brutal, honest perspectives on how you can improve your own "dash" and the "dash" of many others. Doing so will be a journey down a road less traveled—a road that leaves the herd and leads to a new way to advise.

We are not yet dead. We are not at our funeral. Our eulogies haven't been written yet. That means we get to begin now. You may choose to start over. You may choose to continue what you are doing with a newfound energy. Of course you may choose to ignore it all, but I hope you won't.

Stop Doing These Three Things

We need to stop doing certain things. I do not know tomorrow's headlines better than the next guy, but there are three things I'm going to tell you to stop doing right now:

1. Stop talking about the markets.
2. Stop trying to time the market.
3. Stop trying to add value through math or performance.

Instead, look for the truth of history. Find the you in yourself and commit to it. Allow the vision of who you can be unfold. Create the plan to make it happen. From this plan will come strategies and daily tactics to move you forward towards your vision.

Fulfillment of Your Vision

Remember that vision is an act of creation, and I can't explain the mysterious way it works or why I rarely see anything but the next few steps along the path. All I know is that when I've taken the time to develop a vision, it takes on a life of its own and becomes its own self-fulfilling prophecy. I'll set it aside and relax, and suddenly a thought shows up that I know is inspired. It's the process. Life is a process. When you create a vision, a plan will appear. Once you see a plan to meet your Vision, strategies will appear. Once strategies appear, daily activities will fall into place. Don't try to figure it out. Just go with the flow and be amazed at the results.

It is not selfish to try to be successful or to try to be the best *you* possible. You can help more people by adopting a philosophy and a process that allows you to be successful. I want you to be successful in the full meaning of the word, not just financially, but by your own personal definition of success. I cannot tell you what success means in your world, but I have tried to show you how I define it and how I developed a simple process around my philosophy of life that allows not only me, but my clients as well, to achieve success.

When I think about the heart of this book, I realize that what I'm really trying to teach is how to *behave differently*. Life is about deciding what you want and choosing a way to behave that allows you to get what you want in a sustainable way.

The Only Reality That Matters

Jim Carrey's character Truman Burbank in the movie *The Truman Show* has much to teach about my message. If you recall, everything in Truman's life is fabricated. He is, in fact, living in a television show. At the end of the movie, Truman wakes up to a new reality, the actual reality. That is what I'm trying to do with this book. After you read this book, I want you to wake up to the reality that the way most companies and "experts" tell you how to be financial advisors is, in my opinion, not true. It is not right. It does not work. In the end, the client wishes not for more money, but for a better life.

The only reality that matters is knowing what you want, and behaving in a way that allows you to get there. The same is true for your clients. If the financial markets can teach us something about human behavior, it might be that they take from those who lose patience to benefit those who do not. When you choose to be a financial advisor instead of a salesperson, your clients will start to behave differently, too.

Remember, you only have one life to live. My desire is to help you live the one you have in the best way possible, and teach your clients to do the same. As author and lecturer, Marianne Williamson, wrote, "Your playing small doesn't serve the world." Let's make a difference for our clients by investing in the ongoing improvement of mankind's quality of life, one client at a time.

As for the future of the markets, and the concerns you hear daily in the media, I offer you this perspective:

Money Makes Money but the Money Money Makes Makes More. No I did not mistype; this seems to be a fact. You invest your money with the hope to making more. The money you invested plus the money you can potentially make combines to make more. This is the power of compounding. Please grasp this philosophy and never let go. *Money Makes Money but the Money Money Makes Makes More.*

We learn from history that the more money mankind makes, the more money that money creates. Mankind has always sought to improve their quality of life, and there's no reason to think it won't continue. Most who find emotional present-day reasons not to invest in the future improvement in the quality of life miss out on this compounding.

As mankind grows, so grows the opportunity. After World War II, America was one of the few functioning economies on the planet. When you are the only thing going, you can set the rules and enjoy the benefits.

In 1957—right in the midst of the years during which 70 million baby-boomers were born—the S&P was at 47 and US GDP was $466 Billion. Today in mid 2011, the S&P is at 1300 and the US GDP is over $14 Trillion, but many of those baby boomers did not trust their money to the potential for growth thirty years ago, and they continue to make the mistake of saying this growth cannot continue. To make a bet otherwise, as you do when you refuse to invest in this trend, is to bet against mankind.

You see there were 70 million people who wanted to have clothes, food, shelter, transportation and a better life. Well, my fellow advisors, there are about 2,500,000,000 people in China and India today who want what 70 million people wanted in the US over the last 60 years: a better life.

There are just over 300,000,000 people in the US. For every one American, there are about ten Chinese. Of the 300,000,000 US people, the median age is 35. Of the 2,500,000,000 people in China and India the median age is 28. When over a billion people develop a middle class like the baby boomers did over the last 60 years, amazing things will happen. (Source: Wikipedia.com)

Economic growth will happen as human ingenuity seeks to meet the demand of billions of people who not only desire to make a better life for themselves, but they are actually starting to do something to make that happen.

"By 2015, for the first time in 300 years, the number of Asian middle class consumers will equal the number in Europe and North America. By 2021, on present trends, there could be more than two billion Asians in middle class households," say Homi Kharas and Geoffrey Gertz of the Wolfensohn Center for Development at the Brookings Institution.

Speaker and veteran financial advisor Nick Murray says, "Advisors and their clients, seeking an answer to the mystery of why the great companies in America and the world are performing so very much better than the domestic U.S. economy seems to be doing, should pay close attention to this phenomenon, for surely it is the defining macroeconomic trend of the first third (if not more) of the twenty-first century: the exponential growth in the sheer numbers, not to mention the purchasing power, of the middle class outside of the developed world."

As professionals, our job must be to help our clients realize they can either participate in this reality or fall victim to it. Please understand, the people who will benefit from this opportunity are not limited by borders or ethnicities; rather, they are the individuals who invest in the companies that are seeking to meet the demands of a billion new consumers in our global economy. There will be huge swings in the market along the way, as the opportunity for this kind of growth is typically very messy. From 1957 to the present, there have been plenty of reasons not to invest. However, none of those reasons stopped mankind from improving itself and, along the way, creating wealth.

Market Exposure: Need More; Want Less[1]

In my 20 years of investment experience, both personal and professional, I offer you what you need the most: perspective. After all, perspective is truly the one agent that can offer us a studied glance at the big picture and thereby help to keep us on track to our most cherished goals.

The following section is aimed at sharing my philosophy and thoughts in order to pass along to you the perspective we should keep in managing clients' wealth and futures.

---

1 Nick Murray (http://www.nickmurray.com)

As we seek to understand the very important balance of risk vs. return of a portfolio, I am amazed by how often the "risk" is buying what everyone wants and the "return" comes from buying what no one wants and selling it once the herd wants it again. For me, risk vs. return comes down to this question, "How much return can one expect in exchange for a set amount of risk?"

In my opinion, the longer the positive return has already happened in the past, the greater the risk it will have a correction in the future. More importantly, the longer the negative return that has already happened, the lower the risk it will continue to be negative in the future. At the end of the day, if return were not given to those who take risks, nobody would take them.

My example for risk and return is like stretching a rubber band. The more you pull a rubber band, the less potential you have to continue in the direction you are stretching the band. While you stretch it, there is more and more energy building for the rubber band to create momentum to change course and move in the opposite direction. Well, I believe there is a similar relationship between the stock and bond markets. Like the band, they are constantly expanding and contracting, building momentum and energy to go forward and/or change course.

As we research the history of what has happened, it frequently becomes a guide for the future. That research and guide have developed over more than a decade to become my 30-year retirement philosophy. Now, this is not a short-term market prediction, because I have learned not to have short-term market predictions. I only have long-term fundamental philosophies. This is because predictions, especially short-term, change daily and cause many to be wrong. Additionally, philosophies do not often change or need to change as much as they require patience.

Thus, here is my long-term philosophy of my predetermined investment strategy. We will typically maintain an asset allocation of stocks to bonds in a range between 60-80% stocks and 20-40% bonds. Within this asset allocation, we will seek to maximize the stewardship principle of diversification within each asset class. Additionally, we will adjust and rebalance both the asset allocation and diversification within our portfolios as needed. For the next 30 years, we will typically be a lot more invested in stocks than most individuals and retirees may want to own. We do this not to create more volatility and thus more worry in our clients. To the contrary, we do this because we strongly believe we will need to own them in order to have any potential for creating the returns a 30-year retirement will require. We will, for the next several decades, typically own what most people today would not feel comfortable owning. Why? Because if the average person does not want to own it, you can often buy it at a value or a reduced historical price. Furthermore, if the average person wants to buy it, there is often a reduced value or a premium paid over the historical price, which is a risk we seek to avoid.

History is a great teacher here, so let's review a little history most people either do not know or refuse to apply to their investment strategies. This little bit of history is what has made me more optimistic about our future than at any other time in the last 20 years.

Headline: Oct. 31, 2011 (Bloomberg) — The biggest bond gains in almost a decade have pushed returns on Treasuries above stocks over the past 30 years. Bloomberg reported this recent research finding by James Bianco of Bianco Research in Chicago. For the thirty years through September 30th, 2011, long-term government bonds created a compounded return of 11.5%; this was greater than the S&P 500 return during that same time period of 10.8%. The report pointed out a number of factors that qualify this finding. Chief among them was the rise in bond prices due to the slashing of interest rates from the mid-teens in the late 1970s to near zero today.

Fact: Stocks have risen more than bonds over every 30-year period from 1861 until now. (Source: Jeremy Siegel, a finance professor at the University of Pennsylvania's Wharton School in Philadelphia).

Knowing that fact, I am excited about the next 30 years. The next 30 years, which will be defined in history as the Baby Boomers' retirements, might just be the reverse of this recent event not seen since 1861. Simply put, in my opinion, stocks will outperform bonds over the next 30 years.

The fact that there was only one other time in the last 150 years of history where bonds outperformed stocks over a 30 year time frame leads me to believe this and helps me gain perspective in how rare the last 30 year time frame truly was in history.

So, for those who want to continue to not invest in the stock market in the hopes that the last 30 years of bond markets will continue, in our opinion, you are taking a huge risk at the expense of your future income. We believe history will show a 30-year return of the S&P 500 of 10.8% to be more common and that it is not unreasonable to expect in the future.

Therefore, to bring this all together, why are we exposing our clients to more of the market's possibilities than to bonds or fixed income? Because we feel to invest in any bond or fixed income investment going forward carries more risk than reward. With history as our guide, we feel creating a philosophy off of something that hasn't happened since the Civil War era makes for very poor judgment. Also, 30 years from now we would like to reduce the chance you either ran out of retirement income or permanently missed the market advancement. Lastly, at the end of this next 30 years, I am going to retire. In my own transition into retirement, I would hope to hear from you and all our clients on how our advice helped to create a more secure retirement and lasting legacy.

There is an old saying: the exception to the rule proves the rule. Day to day, we need our clients to realize there will be exceptions to our investment strategy. Someone will win the lottery today, if we only had the winning ticket. Every day there will be something else we could do. Tomorrow we will know what performed the best today and wish we had owned more of it.

Hindsight can be overcome by a balanced, time-tested strategy and holding strongly to the fundamental belief that the long-term return will reward those who risk holding a diversified portfolio in some of the best companies around the world.

In closing, I encourage you to file this little book away in a time capsule. Pull it out in a few years. Notice how many bond holders may realize the permanent loss that is created when interest rates go up. Take note of how many people are still waiting for the markets to "get better," all while you have experienced a wonderful historic recovery. I believe this will happen, much to the surprise of CNBC and the investment public.

Impact Your World. It's Your Choice.

Growing demand in this world will create rewarding investment opportunities, and the rewards will help offset the inflation that will be created as a by-product of the demand. Will you and your clients participate? Or will you be victims to this tidal wave? The future of your clients' lives (and your own) can be wonderful memories of all they did and accomplished, or regrets over what was undone or untried. Which one becomes reality is largely based on how you build your practice to help people be better stewards of what they have.

Your playing small does not serve the world. You have an opportunity to impact your world forever. Go make a difference in the lives of your clients one at a time, and in doing so, impact your own life.

APPENDIX:
Children's World Impact Foundation

I don't want your money for myself.

100% of the proceeds from the sale of this book will go directly to the Children's World Impact Foundation (Children's World Impact, Inc.), founded by my wife and me, because we wanted to create an organization where every dollar raised actually goes to the needs of the people it benefits.

In 2000 I was on the board of directors for an organization whose mission was to help children. I quickly realized that their inappropriate resource management minimized how many children could actually be helped. For example, the director was making $100,000 a year to raise $110,000 a year. Only $10,000 was going to the children. So as a board we cleaned house, fixed the budget and created policies to help make sure this could not happen again. After I got off the board of directors, I decide to go start my own foundation.

At the Children's World Impact Foundation, we underwrite all expenses completely so that all individual donations go directly to our projects.

We currently have ongoing projects in Ghana Africa and Haiti. In these countries we seek to financially support women and children by helping make sure they are getting food, clothing, shelter and the medical care they need. Additionally, we are undertaking to do community development work that includes building a school, water purification systems, and homes, all in an effort to keep people from abandoning their children.

The Children's World Impact Foundation will ensure that 100% of the proceeds of this book's sales will go to support vital humanitarian efforts. Together we impact the world.

For more information go to:
www.childrensworldimpact.org

ABOUT THE AUTHOR:

Tyson Jon Ray, CFP®

When Tyson Ray sets out to accomplish something he does it full throttle.

As this book goes to press in 2012, Tyson is Managing Director of Investments for a national financial services company, working in his hometown of Lake Geneva, Wisconsin. He is a Certified Financial Planner™ and a practitioner who focuses his business around individual retirement and estate planning needs.

He manages and coaches his team of two additional partners who are also CFP® professionals, three registered financial associates, and one additional support staff. Together they make a difference in the lives of their family of clients.

Immediately upon graduating from the University of West Florida in Business, Psychology and Political Science in December 1997, Tyson joined a regional firm at the age of 22. By the time he turned 24, he had received the highest award for superior performance and production for a new broker in the first 24 months.

Just a year later, Tyson reached $450,000 in production, entering the President's Council Recognition level.

In early 2001, Tyson became one of the youngest branch managers at his first firm at only 26. He moved a small satellite office—just himself and two other consultants—to another town and built a new office. It was also at this time he found his lovely bride Jenny.

Over the next five years, Tyson added ten additional financial consultants and seven support staff. Under his management, office revenues grew from $600,000 to over $3,000,000. He also made time for seminary master's courses and being a father to his first son, Nelson. He began traveling around the country speaking to other financial advisors about the financial advisory business and practice management.

In addition to branch growth, Tyson grew his own business. At age 29, Tyson was one of the youngest financial advisors at his firm to become a $1,000,000 producer. That same year he was also made an officer of the firm.

After redefining "The Roaring Twenties," Tyson embraced his third decade with energy and action. After turning 30, he welcomed his second son, Austin. In November, 2005, he finished the Florida Ironman held in Panama City. For that event, he formed a special fundraiser called Team IronKids and became one of the top Ironman (triathlon) fundraisers, raising over $50,000 for a local Christian camp for kids.

Never one to rest on the laurels of past accomplishment, and touched by the need of children he observed in travels to third world countries, Tyson decided to establish a charitable foundation.

The Children's World Impact, Inc Foundation seeks to support various missionary and humanitarian efforts around the world and currently has a focus in Haiti. In fall of 2010, the CWI Foundation helped package almost 250,000 meals and distribute them to Haitian orphans. In 2012, the Foundation built a school for 400 children in Haiti, built a mill to help 100 widows in Ghana Africa, and packaged more meals.

Tyson's "Ministry"

Tyson views his business as a ministry devoted to help people be more in control of their finances and their daily lives. He comes alongside his clients with customized strategies designed to preserve, create, manage and distribute wealth through a tailored approach.

It's beautifully simple. He truly has a passion for helping take people where they want to go. He doesn't just care about helping people financially; he really cares about them personally, and that is the secret to his phenomenal success.

Personal Background

Tyson has always been an overachiever. He started working for others when he was 11 years old. At the age of sixteen, he started investing $100 a month from the wages he earned and bought his first stocks before graduating high school. With an instinctive understanding of economics and investment, Tyson has enjoyed following the financial markets for most of his life.

In addition to his consulting career, Tyson is an avid hunter and fisherman. He loves to play golf and exercise.

Tyson married the love of his life, Jenny, in 2001. Jenny is originally from Stevens Point, Wisconsin, and has since retired from her career in law enforcement to devote herself to charitable pursuits and the raising of their three sons, Nelson, Austin and Carson.

Plan Your Life - Manage Your Wealth - Change Your World

www.yourworldimpact.com

27567771R00080

Made in the USA
Lexington, KY
14 November 2013